Randall Heier's book, "Hearing G
Extraordinary Journey of Listenir
journey of what normative New
like according to John 10:27, "M
Randall makes hearing the voice
every believer. If you are hungry for more of Jesus' reality in
your life, read this book.

Dr. Nick Gough, MTS, D. Min
Adjunct Professor, Global Awakening Theological Seminary

Randall Heier's Hearing God's Voice serves as a field guide to those desiring deeper intimacy and encounter with the Triune God. Densely populated with Scripture and through firsthand real-life anecdotes and illustrations, Randall beckons the reader on a journey of discovering how to hear God's voice – both for oneself and others. This read is theologically grounded, invitational, and intentionally experiential, welcoming the reader into new and fresh encounters with the God who speaks. Such a helpful book. As Jesus himself stated, "Man shall not live on bread alone, but on every word that comes from the mouth of God."

Nick Kadun, MAIS
Lead Pastor, Capstone Church

So many believers today do not realize they have the same access to hearing the Father's voice as Jesus did. The same spirit that raised Christ from the dead lives in us meaning we can enjoy the fullness and joy of knowing the Father intimately and hear what He is speaking to us about ourselves and others. Randall Heier does an incredible job of laying this out and demystifying the practice of hearing God's voice. Through his own experiences and skillfully using the Bible, Randall shows that all believers and disciples of Jesus can hear God's voice in any situation.

Joe Sinanan
National Director, Contend Canada

Randall's book on hearing the voice of God is a powerful, yet simple reminder that the Creator God wants to communicate with His people. Randall's use of scripture, relevant stories and multiple references provide a strong backing for the truth that we are all loved by God - and He wants us to hear Him say just that. I highly recommend this book.

Jon Justine
YWAM Missionary and Teacher, Thailand

Randall Heier provides wonderful examples, fresh tools and a clear outline to guide any reader toward greater clarity in listening to and discerning the voice of God. I'm proud to have known and seen Randall apply the truths he writes about; so what is provided is much more than theory - It's tested and tried principles that help us experience the kind of fellowship with Jesus we were designed for.

"Hearing God's Voice: The Extraordinary Journey of Listening to God" stirs hunger and dedication to the idea of walking with the Spirit, in contrast to walking in our own wisdom and understanding. For those who truly desire to acquire practical tools for daily fellowship with Christ, this book provides delightful examples and solid Biblical instruction to guide the reader beyond religiousness and into true relationship with our King.

Kristy Wilke, MA Leadership
YWAM Leader and Worship Pastor of Canvas Church

"In his book, Randall shows us how to walk in the ways and will of God by pointing us to God's timeless Word and offering practical steps to maturity in our faith. Randall's book is a call and invitation for all believers to consistently hear God's voice and powerfully walk in the leading of the Holy Spirit."

Christian Lenty
Founder of The MST Project

Yes, indeed, this isn't just a book. I concur that it is one of the "life messages" of the author, Randall Heier. Typical of his teaching gift, Randall succinctly covers the major themes of "Hearing God's Voice" with the simplicity that an early explorer can understand, but with the depth that will benefit even the most experienced on this journey. There is both sound teaching, combined with an authority of one who has carried this mantle faithfully.

Randall prophetically challenges the reader to go beyond "boring Christianity," to live faith out-of-the-box on the cutting edge of biblical faith and hearing-God-obedience, which inevitably brings a Divine sense of adventure. Goodbye boredom! His writing style is sweetly conversational, warm and affable, a great reflection of the author himself. The chapters conclude with prayer and activation steps, which I personally found very helpful, insightful and catalytic in deepening my journey of hearing His voice. Get ready to be enriched, encouraged and blessed as you read.

Rev. D. Mark Griffin
Executive Director, Global Recordings Network
Canada

Hearing God's Voice

Hearing God's Voice
The Extraordinary Journey of Listening to God

Randall Heier

Hearing God's Voice
The Extraordinary Journey of Listening to God
Copyright © 2024

All Scripture references taken from the English Standard Version unless otherwise noted. The ESV® Bible (The Holy Bible, English Standard Version®). ESV® Text Edition: 2016. Copyright © 2001 by Crossway. Used by permission. All rights reserved.

All rights reserved. No part of this publication may be reproduced, stored in a retrieval system, or transmitted in any form or by any means without the prior permission of the publisher.

www.propelchurchglobal.com
www.randallheier.com

I dedicate this book to my wife, Becky.
Thank you for living this journey with me. Becky, you challenge me and encourage me and I am so glad we are in this together.

To our two daughters, Olivia and Gwenyth.
May you always live your life listening to His voice, may you go further than I have ever gone, taking greater steps of faith, and may He take you on the most extraordinary adventure. I am so proud of you both!

Contents

Introduction..10-18
Chapter 1..19-24
A God Who Speaks
Chapter 2..25-39
Created To Hear His Voice
Chapter 3..40-47
Does God Still Speak Today?
Chapter 4..48-57
God Speaks Through His Written Word
Chapter 5..58-90
Biblical Ways in Which God Speaks
Chapter 6...91-112
Spiritual Gifts
Chapter 7...113-128
The Gift of Prophecy
Chapter 8...129-138
Am I Hearing God?
Chapter 9...139-156
The Good Shepherd
Chapter 10...157-163
Creating an Environment To Hear God's Voice
Chapter 11...164-186
Jesus and the Voice of God
Chapter 12...187-196
Conclusion: The Extraordinary Journey
Appendix...197-203
How to Be Filled With the Holy Spirit
Recommended Reading................................204-206

Introduction

In the Fall of 2020, I served on staff at a church, and we were doing a series of teachings on hearing God's voice. I was asked to preach from John 10, the Good Shepherd. As I preached, I could feel a burning in my heart for this message; it wasn't just another sermon; I sensed it could be much more than that…

After the service, a lady approached me and said, "Randall, you just preached your life's message." I was very encouraged, and felt perhaps God was confirming what I was feeling. As I left the church that day and drove home, I thought about this encouragement and knew that the Lord was speaking to me. When I got home, Becky and I began talking about the morning while eating lunch, and she said, "Randall, after you preached in the first service, I felt like the Lord said to me, "This is his life's message." I was blown away! One of my favourite things about Becky, but sometimes very difficult, is that she is a straight shooter, so I knew she wasn't just blowing smoke. I knew God was confirming what He had just shared with me through the lady at church, and what I had sensed in my spirit. Within an hour, not only had I felt a burning in my heart for this message, but two people had told me that this was my life message! This, in part, is why I am writing this book. It is a message that burns deep within me and has taken my family on a glorious adventure. It is a message that the body of Christ desperately needs to hear and live by.

I had an incredible upbringing in studying and knowing the word of God, and for that, I am forever indebted, but the concept of hearing the voice of God was foreign to me; it was something that I was never taught. In the Winter of 2008, God led me to a Discipleship Training School in Youth With a Mission (YWAM). This decision forever changed my life! During the very first week, my interaction and relation to God was radically altered through a teaching on Hearing the Voice of God by Kristy Wilke. Kristy has spent over 30 years in YWAM and has mobilized thousands of young adults as the Discipleship Training School Director along with her husband Jeff, to go to the nations, sharing the good news of Jesus Christ. YWAM was founded on hearing God's voice and obeying His words and has become the largest mission-sending organization in the world. As Kristy taught she shared story after story of God speaking and walking in obedience to what He said. She explained, "Many think that it is weird or unbiblical to hear God's voice outside of the Bible, but I would argue it is impossible to be the hands and feet of Jesus and not hear His voice."[1]

Over the next four years as I served on staff, through practice and repetition, hearing God's voice and walking in obedience became a part of my DNA. Did I get it right every time? No, but stepping out in faith and trusting God is never a waste. Since marrying my wife, Becky, we vowed to one

---

[1] Kristy Wilke, "Hearing God's Voice," (Lecture Notes, University of the Nations, January 2008).

another that we would live a life devoted to listening to God in every area of our lives. It has been one of the hardest things in my life, and yet the most rewarding thing in my life. He has been faithful in every season to lead us! There is never a dull moment in following His voice! I love the title of Joy Dawson's book "Forever Ruined for the Ordinary." The adventure of hearing and obeying God's voice will never leave you feeling bored. You will forever be ruined for the ordinary.

      God is always speaking; He is always saying something. Sometimes, it is a word about our identity and who we are in Christ. Sometimes, it is about our future and what He is calling us to. Jesus speaks in all areas of our lives. Other times, we will be in a grocery store, and we might hear God's voice for someone else. It truly is an adventure! I believe that most of the church today is bored because they are not hearing God and obeying what He says. One of God's favourite areas of our lives to speak into is our identity. Scripture is filled with verses about our identity in Christ. One time I was leading a seminar on hearing God's voice to a small class of six (don't ever be discouraged about the size of an event, God is present and always wants to speak.) God spoke in profound ways throughout the day. When a family showed up, they looked discouraged and beaten down. After a day of hearing God speak to them, they all left with big smiles on their faces. God had spoken profoundly to their identity. The mother heard God speak so clearly that she was not an "accident." She wept as she received the love and affection of the Father over her life.

What Voice Will You Listen To?

According to a study done in 2007 by Yankelovich Inc.[2], a person sees roughly 5,000 ads a day. This study is long outdated, but the point remains the same; we are bombarded with voices all day long. Not only do we see more than 5,000 ads a day, but we also see Facebook, Instagram, X (previously known as Twitter), and the news; we also hear speeches from politicians and doctors, and have conversations with friends, family, and co-workers. These are all voices that bombard our minds, thoughts, and lives. The most critical voice we have yet to mention is the voice of Jesus. In all the noise, how do we tune our ears to Him? How can we recognize that He is speaking to us all the time? How can we yield to Him in all areas of life? How can we fulfill His mandate and call on our lives?

The Future of the Church

I remember going to church in my teenage years and thinking, "there has got to be more than this…" I was bored. The Christian life has to be more than just warming a pew Sunday after Sunday, or singing a few songs and hearing a sermon. IT IS FAR MORE! God is raising up a generation that will no longer tolerate and settle for the mundane Christian life or a church service. They are done with good ideas and plans of man, and truly want to know what God wants, only moving forward when they have heard Him speak. What if we woke up every day with a new assignment from the Lord? That sounds far from boring, and more like an adventure! Allow me to be

---

[2] Mary Atamaniuk, "How Many Ads Do You Actually See Daily?!" Clario, clario.co/blog/ads-seen-daily, Apr 21, 2021

blunt; if you are bored with your walk with God, it's not God, it's you. God has more for your life than you could ever think or imagine! My friend and former leader, Kristy Wilke, said, "Formulas are out; humility says, I will wait on you."[3] I couldn't agree more! Doing what we have done for the last fifty years is out. Doing what we have done for the last 5 or 10 years is out, unless the Lord says it. Allow me to be clear, I'm not talking about removing sound doctrine, solid biblical teaching, communion, evangelism, and the foundations of the faith, I'm talking about how we carry out the Christian faith and our plans and strategies. If we want to bring the Kingdom of God to this earth, we must be a people on the cutting edge of what God is doing and saying. How do we do this? By listening to His voice. We live in a time when it is imperative to hear and obey. We must listen to the Lord for strategies for today rather than what worked 5 years ago; walking in the strategies and wisdom of the kingdom of God, rather than the kingdoms of this world. It is time for the heavens to be opened and the word of the Lord to fall into our hearts. It is time that we say along Jesus, I only do what I see the Father in heaven doing.

John 5:19-20, *"So Jesus said to them, "Truly, truly, I say to you, the Son can do nothing of his own accord, but only what he sees the Father doing. For whatever the Father does, that the Son does likewise. For the Father loves the Son and shows him all that he himself is doing. And greater works than these will he show him, so that you may marvel."*

---

[3] Kristy Wilke, "Hearing God's Voice" (Lecture Notes, University of the Nations, July, 2008).

For years, the Western church has been stuck. Stuck might be a polite way of saying it. Don't take my word for it; individuals who are far more intelligent than myself have been tracking the trends in the West concerning the church, and it is no secret the church is in trouble. Significant decline, mass exodus, and church closures. I cannot help but think it is because we have closed our ears to the voice of God, and we continue to do the same thing year in and year out. Not only are churches closing, but whole denominations are simply ceasing to exist. We like control, we want to know what the future will hold, we like our systems and strategies, and we don't like surprises. What if this is why we see the church in the West in major decline? The church has become primarily irrelevant in our culture. If you read the book of Acts in the Bible, crazy things are happening all the time; the power of the Holy Spirit flowing through the church, there are radical demonstrations of healing, and people are being set free from demonic oppression. The church in evangelical Christianity today has been toned down to four songs and a sermon. Whatever happened to *"these men have turned the world upside down?"* (Acts 17:6) We believe in a God who sent His Son to the earth to die on the cross; He did, and He came back to life three days later! We believe in a God who spoke the world into existence; the beginning and end of our faith cannot just be going to church on Sunday and being half entertained. As I read through the gospels and the New Testament, I can't help but wonder, "why is none of this a reality in our churches, homes, cities and nations today? Why are we not turning the world upside down?"

There is More

Missionary to the Middle East, Dan Bauman says, "The more you give your life to Jesus, the more Jesus has for you beyond what you can even imagine."[4] The Apostle Paul believes and prays for the very same thing;

Ephesians 3:20-21: *"Now to him who is able to do far more abundantly than all that we ask or think, according to the power at work within us, to him be glory in the church and in Christ Jesus throughout all generations, forever and ever. Amen."*

Jesus has so much more for us in our journey with Him. Most of us are thinking too small for the things that God has planned for us since before the foundations of the earth. (Eph 1:4) He has incredible things that He desires to do in and through us. He wants to take us to a hurting and dying world. As we wait upon Him, listen to His voice and walk in quick obedience, there is no telling as to how God will move!

Hearing God's voice and obeying is a journey of faith. As I think about the idea of faith and what it looks like in the life of a Christian, Hebrews 11 comes to mind. There is a reason why it is referred to as the faith chapter, as it talks about all the heroes of the faith who heard God and obeyed Him. They all had to exude enormous faith! Our family has taken many of our own leaps of faith, believing in the Lord for

---

[4] Dan Bauman, "Missions" (Lecture Notes, University of the Nations, February, 2008)

incredible things, and I am excited to share some of our journey with you! The in-between is the difficult part. The land between the promise and the fulfillment of that promise. This is the space where you need to know where you are going. You can't see the end; all you can do is trust the Lord. This is the part that is pleasing to God.

Hebrews 11:6 says, *"And without faith, it is impossible to please him, for whoever would draw near to God must believe that he exists and that he rewards those who seek him."*

Fear will often accompany steps of faith. What happens if God doesn't come through? What if I got it wrong? I want to encourage you; you can never have too much faith in God or believe in something too big. God isn't looking down from heaven and saying, "Oh no, Randall is exerting too much faith. I don't think I'll be able to come through on that big of a promise." At the same time, the faith journey will rarely turn out like we think it will. There will be incredible seasons of difficulty and reward. We will go places we never thought of or imagined. We will go through seasons and storms that we wouldn't wish upon our greatest enemies. We will go through trials that hurt us and prune us. This is all a part of the adventure the Lord is inviting us on!

Referring to Paul's famous prayer in Ephesians 3, he prays, *"Now to him who is able to do far more abundantly than all that we ask or think, according to the power at work within us."* If you are willing to be a pioneer, look foolish and do life in a completely different way, then you are ready to go on the most glorious journey ever. God will lead you into things you only dreamed of. God will sovereignly align relationships you thought were impossible in the natural world, and will open up doors that were not even on your radar. Hold on and get ready.

<u>Prayer:</u>

God, I step into all that you have for me. I ask that you take me on a journey into the great unknown. Take me into great steps of faith and obedience in the days, months and years ahead. Give me the grace to hear your voice and walk in quick obedience. I declare that the Christian life is not boring. God you are not boring!

Chapter 1
A God Who Speaks

Tell him, "Your sister is safe." I had a pit in my stomach, while waiting in line at the store, and I felt like the Lord was telling me that the teller was worried about his sister and that she was okay; he didn't have to worry anymore. As I got to the checkout, I paid for my things and then turned back to him. I said, "Hey, this might sound weird, but I believe in God, and I have a relationship with Him; sometimes, He tells me things to tell others." I then asked him if he had a sister, and he did. YES! I had heard God correctly on that. I said, "Jesus wants you to know that your sister is safe, and you don't have to worry about her." He looked at me with a big smile and said, "My sister lives back home in India, and the rest of our family is here in Alberta, Canada. We constantly worry about her, and I talk with her every day to ensure she is okay. She has a boyfriend that isn't a good influence on her." I looked at him and said, "God wants you to know that He loves and cares about you, and is concerned with the details of your life." Although this young man did not give his life to Jesus at that moment, he had an encounter with a living God; a God who desires to speak to him and who wants to be in a relationship with him. This is the God we serve.

At the core of the Christian faith, we believe in a God who communicates. If you think about it, the scriptures are records of God communicating to His people.

2 Peter 1:21: *"For no prophecy was ever produced by the will of man, but men spoke from God as they were carried along by the Holy Spirit."*

Not only that, God spoke the world and all of creation into existence.

Psalm 33:6: *"By the word of the Lord, the heavens were made, and by the breath of his mouth all their host."*
Hebrews 1:3: "He is the radiance of the glory of God and the exact imprint of his nature, and he upholds the universe by the word of his power."

Isn't this fascinating? Think about this for a moment. God spoke, and the world took shape. God spoke, and light began to shine. God spoke, and trees began to grow. God spoke, and rivers began to flow. The book of Genesis is a book of beginnings, and we see God speak a lot throughout it. God spoke with Adam and Eve in the Garden (Genesis 3:8), the very first humans to live on the earth. God spoke to Noah to build an ark and lead his family to safety (Genesis 6-9). God talked to Abraham, Isaac and Jacob, the three Patriarchs of the faith, in many different ways: dreams, visions, and through angels. Moses communed with God on many occasions and was given incredible direction for the Israelite people as they were set free from slavery in Egypt. Not only did God speak with them, Abraham and Moses were considered friends of God (Isaiah 41:8, 33:11). We have only scratched the surface of the examples of God speaking with different people throughout the Bible. Books upon books could be written about all the conversations between God and individuals of ages past. We haven't even touched on God speaking to Joseph in multiple dreams and receiving the interpretation of the dreams of others (Genesis 37-50). God spoke to Samuel in the night (1 Samuel 3), and Isaiah heard the still small voice (1 Kings 19:12-13). All the prophets of old heard from God to bring comfort and correction to the Israelites. The New Testament is chalked full of examples as well. God speaks to Mary through an angel in the night and her husband, Joseph (Luke 1, Matthew 1). God says in an audible voice at the baptism of Jesus, *"This is my son with whom I am well pleased"* (Matthew 3). The apostle Paul has many encounters with the Lord in the book of Acts. The final letter in the Bible (Revelation) was a vision God gave to John.

    There is no beating around the proverbial bush; when we read the Bible, we are confronted with a God who speaks. The phrase "God said" or "God spoke" is written over a thousand times in the Scriptures. There is simply no dancing around it; God speaks! I love what Darlene Cunningham (the co-founder of YWAM) says, "God is an amazing communicator. The most common phrases in the Bible are God said, or the Lord said."[5]

---

[5] Darlene Cunningham, Values Matter (Seattle, WA: YWAM Publishing, 2020), 50-51

Not only does God speak, but He cares deeply about His creation. He longs to be in a relationship with each one of us. His desire for a relationship with us is why He sent His son Jesus to earth, to die on the cross, and to be raised to life, so that all who are followers of Him might have eternal life!

He is also a God of incredible detail, He cares about matters big and small, and His thoughts towards us are many.

Matthew 10:30: *"But even the hairs of your head are all numbered."*
Psalm 139:17-18: *"How precious to me are your thoughts, O God! How vast is the sum of them! If I would count them, they are more than the sand. I awake, and I am still with you."*

Before I knew Becky, she was shopping for a gift for her friend's wedding. She came across an item she wanted to purchase that came in two different colours: brown and purple. Standing in the store, she asked the Lord, "God, what colour should I get?" She felt like the Lord said purple. After giving the gift to her friend, she asked her what colour she would have chosen, and knowing that Becky was learning to hear God's voice, she honestly answered, "purple."

Our God desires to be involved in the smallest details of our lives, not because He is controlling, but because He loves the people He created and desires to speak with them. God is so faithful and He tells us that He will speak to us:

Jeremiah 33:3: *"Call to me, and I will answer you and will tell you great and hidden things that you have not known."*

Brad Jersak calls this verse God's phone number, he shares this wonderful idea that throughout the scripture, God has many definitive statements; one of those statements is found in Jeremiah 33:3, "I will answer."[6] How encouraging and comforting is this promise? We don't have to wonder or worry if God will speak to us; He has definitively promised us in scripture! The writer of Deuteronomy also points to our God who speaks.

Deuteronomy 4:7: *"For what great nation is there that has a god so near to it as the Lord our God is to us, whenever we call upon him?"*

Every summer since I met my wife, Becky, we have spent a week in British Columbia, Canada with her family at a condo. These times are usually spent visiting with family, swimming at the pool, meeting new people, reading, and relaxing. One summer, we got to know a family quite well, as we spent almost every day at the pool with them. Near the end of the week, I began to pray for the wife as I could tell she had a colourful past. I began to feel a burden in my heart for her. As I was praying for her, a picture flashed through my mind; I saw her as a young girl in a sundress and a wide-brimmed hat; she was crying with disappointment. Although I didn't see or feel any specific disappointment, I knew it was disappointment that stretched across the entirety of her life. As I continued to pray for her, I felt the Holy Spirit's prompting to share this picture

---

[6] Brad Jersak, can you hear me? (Abbotsford, BC: Fresh Wind Press, 2012), 28

with her and to tell her that if she brought her disappointment to Jesus, He would heal her. Becky was chatting with her, so I walked over to them and said, "This might sound weird, but I have a relationship with God, and I believe He shares things with me for others sometimes. Do you mind if I tell you what He has shared with me about you?" She was super open to hearing what God would say to her, and as I shared the picture with her, tears began to stream down her face. As she began to respond, she couldn't wipe her tears away fast enough, they just kept coming. "Randall, I have more disappointment than you could imagine; I don't even know where to begin." I told her, if she were willing to give it to Jesus, He would take it from her and heal her. She wasn't too interested in God; you could tell she had some walls up, but we both knew she had encountered Him. This led to a conversation that would be far too long for this book, but the point is that God is so radically in love with His creation that He wants to be in a relationship with each one of us.

We serve an incredible God who knows all the details of our lives and longs to be in a relationship with us. He is a God who is not silent, but speaks loud and clear.

<u>Prayer:</u>
God, I pray that you would open the ears of my heart to hear your voice. I thank you that you are a God who is not silent or distant, but you are near to each one of us.

<u>Activation:</u>
Put your hand over your heart and declare, "I will hear the voice of the Lord today."

Chapter 2
Created to Hear His Voice

"Some people think it's weird that we can hear the voice of God. Weird would be to presume we can operate and minister without it."[7] - Kristy Wilke

If you have been in the church for some time or have been a believer most of your life, you will know that all "good Christians" have a quiet time. Set your clock for 6 a.m., pull yourself out of bed, make your way over to the kitchen table or recliner, open your Bible to your bookmark, read for fifteen minutes and boom. Done. "I have spent my time with the Lord." Now, hear my heart; please don't think that you no longer need to read your Bible by what I am about to say. Do you think that the God of the universe, the one who spoke the world into being, defines a relationship with His people as reading the Bible for fifteen minutes everyday? We are made for so much more than this! We are created to hear His voice and walk in an intimate relationship with Him.

---

[7] Kristy Wilke, "Hearing God's Voice"

Created with a Body

When God created Adam and Eve, He made them with three different parts—spirit, soul and body. Jack Hayford calls our body "the part of us that is world-conscious, the soul is the part of us that is self-conscious, and our spirit is the part of us that is God-conscious."[8] Your body consists of your arms, legs, muscles, bones, tendons, and many other parts. We have been given five primary senses: sight, taste, hearing, smell, and touch or feeling. We live in the physical realm, the world God created. We live in houses, drive around in cars, and go to work. We live in the created material world. When God created humans in the garden, He made them good (Genesis 1:26-31). Therefore, it means that our bodies are good. Many of us are ashamed of our bodies, we believe we are ugly or our bodies are ugly, however listen to the words of King David.

Psalm 139:14: *"I praise you, for I am fearfully and wonderfully made. Wonderful are your works; my soul knows it very well."*

David praises the Lord for the great care God took in making each one of us. He created each one of us unique.

---

[8] Jack Hayford, "Hayford Bible Handbook" (Nashville, Tennessee: Thomas Nelson, 2004) 788

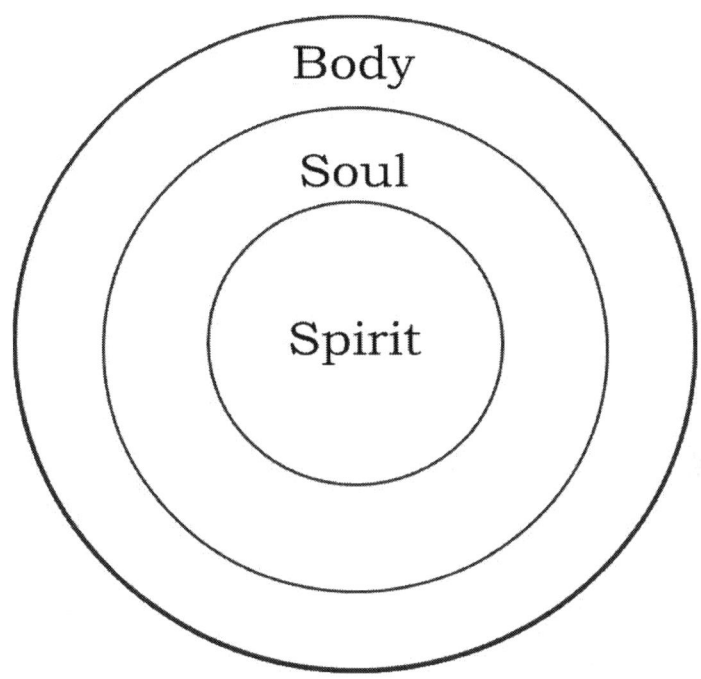

Created with a Soul

God also created us with a soul. The soul is made up of our mind, will and emotions. It also contains our imagination, reasoning, and intellect. The soul is part of your innermost being, the core of who you are, your personality. In Matthew 22:37, Jesus states that we are to love the Lord our God with our heart, soul and mind. Paul states that we need to have our souls renewed.

Romans 12:1-2: *"I appeal to you therefore, brothers, by the mercies of God, to present your bodies as a living sacrifice, holy and acceptable to God, which is your spiritual worship. Do not be conformed to this world, but be transformed by the* *renewal of your mind, that by testing you may discern what is the will of God, what is good and acceptable and perfect."*

The soul and the spirit are so closely connected it is often hard to distinguish between the two. Paul speaks of our inner man in Ephesians 3:14-21 needing to be strengthened. Our inner man is the core of who we are.

Created with a Spirit

The Bible clearly communicates that God has created us with a spirit. It is imperative to know first that God is Spirit.

Genesis 1:1-2: *"In the beginning, God created the heavens and the earth. Now the earth was formless and empty, darkness was over the surface of the deep, and the Spirit of God was hovering over the waters."*

2 Corinthians 3:18: *"And we all, with unveiled face, beholding the glory of the Lord, are being transformed into the same image from one degree of glory to another. For this comes from the Lord, who is the Spirit."*

John 4:24: *"God is Spirit, and those who worship him must worship in spirit and truth."*

Pastor Witness Lee writes this of the creation of man: "Genesis 2:7 unveils the creation of man. God used the dust of the ground to form a body. Then God breathed into the nostrils of this body of dust the breath of life. Proverbs 20:27 says, "The spirit of man is the lamp of Jehovah, Searching all the innermost parts." The Hebrew word for spirit in this verse is the very word for breath in Genesis 2:7. The word commonly used in Hebrew for spirit is ruach, but here in Proverbs 20:27, the Hebrew word for spirit is neshamah, not ruach. This is the same word used for breath in Genesis 2:7. This verse is a strong word to prove that the breath of life which was breathed into the nostrils of man's body of dust at the time of creation is our spirit. Job 32:8 tells us also that there is a spirit in man.[9]

God is Spirit, and He has created us in His image.

Genesis 1:26: *"So God created man in his own image, in the image of God he created him; male and female he created them."*

The way we commune with God is Spirit to spirit and the way we worship God is spirit to Spirit. I love what Jennifer Leclaire, Senior Leader of Awakening House of Prayer says, "If we are created spirit, and God is a Spirit, then our goal is to develop our spirit man."[10] The written word of God does not shy away from telling us how we are created.

1 Thessalonians 5:23: *"Now may the God of peace himself sanctify you completely, and may your whole spirit and soul and body be kept blameless at the coming of our Lord Jesus Christ."*

---

[9] Witness Lee, "Our Human Spirit," Living Stream Ministry, June 5, 2023 *www.ministrysamples.org/excerpts/ANOTHER-SPIRIT.HTML*

[10] Jennifer Leclaire, The Seer (Shippensburg, PA: Destiny Image Publishing, 2019) 31

If God is Spirit and has made us with a spirit, He has given us the unique ability that no other part of His creation has to commune with Him. Many have compared it to radio frequencies. As you scan the tuner of your radio, all you hear is static until you find the correct frequencies. Spirit to spirit; deep crying out to deep (Psalm 42:7).

Emma Stark, 4th generation Bible teacher, communicating in her Celtic boldness clearly states, "God breathed in you: you are not a physical being looking for a spiritual experience. You are a spirit being having a temporary, physical experience."[11] She says, "God is known in the spirit; He is Spirit. Or, to put it more bluntly, God is only truly known in the spirit realm."[12]

We desperately need a revelation that we are not just a body and soul, but spirit, soul and body. We often focus far too much on the physical realm when we should be communicating with God Spirit to spirit.

Romans 8:5-9: *"For those who live according to the flesh set their minds on the things of the flesh, but those who live according to the Spirit set their minds on the things of the Spirit. For to set the mind on the flesh is death, but to set the mind on the Spirit is life and peace."*

---

[11] Emma Stark, The Prophetic Warrior (Shippensburg, PA. Destiny Image, 2020) 177

[12] Stark, The Prophetic Warrior, 180

Created to Hear

You have the innate ability to hear the voice of God. Because you have a spirit, you are hardwired to hear His voice. Jesus speaks comforting words about those who follow Him hearing His voice.

John 8:47: *"Whoever is of God hears the words of God."*
John 18:37: *"Everyone who is of the truth listens to my voice."*
John 10:2-3: *"But he who enters by the door is the shepherd of the sheep. To him, the gatekeeper opens. The sheep hear his voice, and he calls his own sheep by name and leads them out."*

The question is, "Are we listening to His voice?" This requires action on our part. Moment by moment, are you tuning into the Spirit of God and saying, "What do you want to say to me?"

In his book Hearing God, Peter Lord states that there is a beginning point to hearing God. He points to Jesus saying *"He who has ears, let him hear."*[13] Essentially, there must be a willingness and a desire to hear His voice. If we are going to commune with God, hear, understand, and obey Him, we must have the desire.

---

[13] Peter Lord, Hearing God (Grand Rapids, Michigan: Baker Book House Company, 1988) 28

Friendship with God

In my early twenties, I had the privilege of working for a non-profit mission organization called Youth With a Mission (YWAM). I owe a debt of gratitude to the leaders who mentored me and walked alongside me in those years. Much of who I am today is because of them. One of the foundational teachings and values was listening to the voice of God. It radically altered my life and laid the foundation for how my wife and I live today. Walking across the campus parking lot one day, I asked the Lord a question. At this time, I was twenty-one years old, very insecure, and had self-image issues that stemmed from childhood hurts. As I neared the grass outside the cafeteria, I asked the Lord, "What would you like to say to me?" Immediately, without any hesitation, I heard the Lord say, "Randall, I love you." I quickly replied, " When will you tell me something different?" (I had been hearing Jesus tell me this often.) The Lord responded so clearly to my spirit, that to this day, it is one of the most explicit times I have ever heard Him speak. "When you begin to believe that I love you." It was like a bullet in my chest. Jesus had spoken.

Our God loves His children and desires to walk in a relationship with them. He is not distant or angry with us, but eagerly desires to be involved in our lives. As I previously said, we are created for much more than a fifteen-minute quiet time. We are created for friendship with God. This concept is pretty foreign for many in the evangelical church of the West, even though Jesus states this very truth. We so desperately need to understand that God considers us friends.

John 15:15: *"No longer do I call you servants, for the servant does not know what his master is doing; but I have called you friends, for all that I have heard from my Father I have made known to you."*

Paul picks up on this glorious truth and writes about it in his magnum opus to the Romans.

Romans 5:11: (NLT) *"So now we can rejoice in our wonderful new relationship with God because our Lord Jesus Christ has made us friends of God."*

Isn't this astonishing?! We have been made friends of God. Think about your best friend for a moment. Maybe it is your spouse, a co-worker or a classmate; perhaps it is a brother or sister. Whoever it is, you probably know them quite well; you probably know their favourite food and TV show or hobby, and at times, you can finish their sentences and talk for hours on end. One of my closest friends lives about an hour drive from me. We see each other 4 or 5 times a year, but every time we go for coffee, we talk for hours and have to end the conversation multiple times before we actually say goodbye. We laugh and share deep things in our hearts: our struggles, failures, and successes. Even though we can have these incredible friendships on earth, we can be even more personal with God because we know that no matter what, He will never leave us or forsake us, He will not reject us and He will be with us until the end of the age (Hebrews 13:5, Matthew 28:20). My former leader and friend, Kristy Wilke, says, "Friends care about what friends care about."[14] The Lord cares about the things that are on our hearts, and we should, in return, care about the things that are on His heart. Even better, He desires to share the things in His heart with us if we are willing to take the time to listen. Intimacy is marked by listening and speaking; it is about giving and receiving. It is about walking in friendship with God.

The psalmist speaks comforting words about how the Lord knows His children intimately; He even knows our thoughts.

Psalm 139:2-3: *"You know when I sit down and when I rise up; you discern my thoughts from afar. You search out my path and my lying down and are acquainted with all my ways."*

Joy Dawson, former YWAM leader and international speaker, beautifully states that the Lord is intimately acquainted with us. "I believe part of God's unparalleled greatness is His desire and ability to be intimately involved in the smallest details of the lives of billions of the creatures He created and to be communicating to them all at one time, if necessary, in precisely the way and timing that serve their best interests and in their native language."[15]

In the book of Exodus we read about the leader of the people of God, Moses, being a friend of God.

---

[14] Wilke, "Hearing God's Voice"

[15] Joy Dawson, Forever Ruined for the Ordinary (Nashville, Tennessee: Thomas Nelson Publishers, 2001) 7

Exodus 33:9-11: *"When Moses entered the tent, the pillar of cloud would descend and stand at the entrance of the tent, and the Lord would speak with Moses. And when all the people saw the pillar of cloud standing at the entrance of the tent, all the people would rise up and worship, each at his tent door. Thus the Lord used to speak to Moses face to face, as a man speaks to his friend."*

Friendship with God isn't a flippant idea, but it is a reality. God is calling those who follow Him to be friends with Him. Dan Bauman says when Jesus called His disciples, "the call to discipleship was first and foremost an invitation to intimate friendship."[16] When God draws humanity to Himself, He calls them to an intimate friendship with Him, any contentment in this life will come by being satisfied in Jesus alone.

Creating a God Awareness

There are certain things in life that you can learn with your mind, and it forever changes the way you look at things. Other times, you can learn and learn and learn and never really "know." One of these things is having a God awareness. What I mean by "a God awareness" is, theologically, we "know" that the Holy Spirit lives within us, but for most, it is a fluffy truth that doesn't mean much. We must have a revelation that the Holy Spirit lives in us and was given to us so that we can live victorious lives over sin (Galatians 5:22-23), walk in

---

[16] Dan Bauman, A Beautiful Way (Seattle, WA: YWAM Publishing, 2005) 62

righteousness, and walk in His power and the boldness He provides (Acts 1:8). *We must create a God awareness in our lives.* The easiest way to do this is by engaging the Spirit of God wherever you are. You may be reading this on a bus, at your kitchen table or in a library; wherever you are, begin to engage the Spirit of God living inside of you. "Holy Spirit, I love you. Thank you for being in this place. Thank you that you live inside of me. Right now, I choose to engage in a conversation with you. You know my innermost thoughts. Holy Spirit, what do you want to say to me right now?" Pause. Listen. What is coming to your mind?

Having conversations like this with the Holy Spirit in every context of your life will radically alter your "God awareness." You will begin to see Him moving, and you will start to hear Him speaking all the time.

Near the end of Jesus' earthly ministry, He made His disciples aware that He would not be with them much longer, however, He did not leave them without any hope.

John 16:7-11: *"Nevertheless, I tell you the truth: it is to your advantage that I go away, for if I do not go away, the Helper will not come to you. But if I go, I will send him to you." I can imagine the disciples thinking, "Really? Jesus, we don't think you should leave us. It would be better for you to stay; we are just getting started."*

It was to their advantage (and all who follow Jesus) that He would go to heaven. The Father was then able to send the Spirit of Jesus to live in us for our benefit, to empower us for life and ministry. This is a glorious reality. What a beautiful gift. I remember the first time I realized this truth. In the Winter of 2010, Becky and I lived in a small apartment in Montana. I was sitting on our couch reading through the gospel of John. I got to John 16, and my world exploded. For the first time, I believed it was better for Jesus to go to heaven and the Holy Spirit to come. The Holy Spirit now takes up residence in my inner being. If you confess Christ as the King of Kings and Lord of Lords, that He is the Saviour of the world, the son of the living God, you have the Holy Spirit given to you as a promised inheritance.

Luke 11:13: *"If you then, who are evil, know how to give good gifts to your children, how much more will the heavenly Father give the Holy Spirit to those who ask him!"*

The Holy Spirit Himself is a good gift from the Father. The power that raised Jesus from the dead now lives in each of us! Meditate on that!

Romans 8:11: *"If the Spirit of him who raised Jesus from the dead dwells in you, he who raised Christ Jesus from the dead will also give life to your mortal bodies through his Spirit who dwells in you."*

I have heard it said that we are a walking encounter. Everyone we see and come into contact with can encounter God because He lives inside us. This should radically alter the way we go about our days. In the context of hearing God's voice and creating a God awareness, when we intentionally listen to God, and consciously engage with the Spirit of God who lives in us, we hear God more, we become aware that He is always with us. Graham Cooke says, "When we do by intention what you've done by intuition, you achieve acceleration."[17] Meaning, when we intentionally listen to God, we will recognize His voice in all situations. We become aware that wherever we are, the power that raised Jesus from the dead lives in us, and we then have the boldness to pray for someone's healing in the grocery store, or we share an insight into someone's life that we could have only known by the Spirit sharing it with us. We begin to see life differently, the narrative shifts, and we begin releasing the kingdom of God wherever we go. Now, we are pulling the kingdom realities into our world. We are praying *thy kingdom come, thy will be done on earth as it is in heaven*, and seeing the Kingdom of God established in our midst.

    When we listen to Jesus with intention, there is now the opportunity for a dialogue with Him, and a new world of intimacy is opened to us. Over many years, I have begun to grow in intimacy with the Holy Spirit, through the discipline of praying short prayers throughout the day. Now I will be walking through a store, and short prayers begin to flow out of me; I have grown in my God-awareness.

Here are five short prayers that I pray multiple times a day:

Short Prayers to Pray:
Holy Spirit, thank you for living inside of me.

---

[17] Dan Mccallom, Bethel School of the Prophets, (Lecture Notes, Redding, California, August, 2022)

Holy Spirit, explode out of me.
Holy Spirit, I love you.
Holy Spirit, make Jesus real to me.
Holy Spirit, I honour you.
Jesus, be seated on the throne of my heart.

Prayer:

God, I thank you that you are everywhere. I thank you that you are inside of me, living and moving. I engage my spirit to communicate with you. I ask that you speak to me loud and clear throughout my day.

Activation:

Followers of Jesus are known to say, "I'm not religious, but I have a relationship with God." This is true of the Christian faith; we have a relationship with the God of the universe. However, many of us spend fifteen minutes reading the Bible daily, which is the extent of our relationship.

A few things that I have done to create a God awareness and pursue a relationship with God are:

1) Set a timer on my watch or phone for specific times throughout the day. When the timer goes off, engage the Holy Spirit in conversation.

2) Put a nickel in my shoe. Years ago, a friend and mentor told me to put a coin in my shoe, and every time I felt it, talk to God.

Chapter 3
Does God Still Speak Today?

Many ask, "does God still speak today?" My friend Kristy says, "Hearing God today outside of His written word is often looked at as weird or unbiblical. But I believe it is weird to think we can exist in this life as His hands and feet and not hear His voice."[18]

The doctrine of cessationism says that God stopped speaking, and the gifts of the Spirit stopped operating when the Bible was finished being written or when the apostles died. International speaker Kim Maas states, "The basic premise of cessationism is that the supernatural workings or gifts of the Spirit served only one purpose: to authenticate the authority of Jesus, the apostles and doctrine. Jesus has ascended to heaven; the New Testament apostles have all died; the Scriptures are complete, and no new writings will be added to the canon."[19] Some point to this passage in Revelation to prove that God does not speak outside of the Bible today:

---

[18] Wilke, Hearing God's Voice

[19] Kim Maas, Prophetic Community (Minneapolis, Minnesota: Chosen, 2019) 68

Revelation 22:18: *"I warn everyone who hears the words of the prophecy of this book: if anyone adds to them, God will add to him the plagues described in this book, 19 and if anyone takes away from the words of the book of this prophecy, God will take away his share in the tree of life and in the holy city, which are described in this book."*

Brad Jersak states that the doctrine of cessationism is manmade and that it locks God in a box. "Over the history of the church, cessationists have used John's warning as a hammer to lock God into a Bible-sized box in which His voice is forever confined. They have created a doctrine that God only speaks from within that box."[20] When God only speaks in one way it is easier to control Him, it is "easier" to do life and ministry in our own way.

Cessationists also point to Paul's writing in his letter to the Corinthians.

1 Corinthians 13:8-12: *"Love never ends. As for prophecies, they will pass away; as for tongues, they will cease; as for knowledge, it will pass away. For we know in part and we prophesy in part, but when the **perfect** comes, the partial will pass away. When I was a child, I spoke like a child, I thought like a child, I reasoned like a child. When I became a man, I gave up childish ways. For now we see in a mirror dimly, but then face to face. Now I know in part; then I shall know fully, even as I have been fully known."*

---

[20] Jersak, can you hear me? 43

Those who believe that the gifts of the Spirit have ceased and that God no longer speaks are gravely mistaken. What Paul is communicating in 1 Corinthians 13:8-12 is when Jesus <u>returns</u> (not when the Bible is completed) the gifts will pass away, there will be no more need for them. We will be forever united with Christ. (1 Thessalonians 4:17)

Jesus, and the New Testament authors do not teach cessationism at all. Jesus is adamant that His sheep hear His voice.

John 10:2-5: *"But he who enters by the door is the shepherd of the sheep. To him the gatekeeper opens. The sheep hear his voice, and he calls his own sheep by name and leads them out. When he has brought out all his own, he goes before them, and the sheep follow him, for they know his voice. A stranger they will not follow, but they will flee from him, for they do not know the voice of strangers."*

Jesus uses a tremendous shepherding analogy to speak about the relationship between Him and His followers. When shepherds call their sheep, they come running to the shepherd. If you have never seen this in person, I recommend finding a video of a shepherd calling their sheep online. It is fascinating. A stranger can dress up in the exact clothing, put on a disguise and use the same call, but the sheep will not budge. They will run away. The sheep intimately know their shepherd's voice. I love how Jesus is so unwavering about His followers hearing His voice. He is not wishy-washy on this idea, because it is true. Jesus is the Good Shepherd; He is our perfect leader, and we will know the voice of our leader.

After fourteen years of marriage, I know my wife's voice better than anyone else's, and by the sound of her voice, I know whether she is sad, upset, anxious or relaxed. Jesus states that His sheep <u>KNOW</u> His voice. Some might think, "Oh yeah, God speaks, just not to me." We might think He only speaks to pastors, elders or really spiritual people, but the fact is that He speaks to His sheep; those who listen.

The Helper

Jesus said that the Holy Spirit would be the one helping us after He ascended into heaven.

John 14:26: *"But the Helper, the Holy Spirit, whom the Father will send in my name, he will teach you all things and bring to your remembrance all that I have said to you."*

Don't Jesus' words not point to the fact that Jesus, by His Spirit, will speak to us? If He doesn't speak to us, how could He teach us or bring to remembrance the words that Jesus said in the first place?

John 16:13: *"When the Spirit of truth comes, he will guide you into all the truth, for he will not speak on his own authority, but whatever he hears he will speak, and he will declare to you the things that are to come."*

We are dependent upon the Spirit to be led into the truth. This should encourage, excite and strengthen us. How do we think we could live out what God has called us to and not hear His voice? This quite frankly is a form of pride and self-dependence. Life in the Kingdom of God cannot be learned just by reading your Bible or reading a book about the Bible, we are spiritual beings who must be led by the Spirit of God. Now, before you close this book and disregard its contents, you should know that I fully believe in God speaking through His written word and it is a major focus in the pages to come.

God is Still Speaking

God is still speaking today; there is no doubt about it. You are likely already hearing God in many ways; you just may not recognize it. The fact that you are a believer of Jesus means you <u>have</u> heard His voice.

John 6:44: *"No one can come to me unless the Father who sent me draws him. And I will raise him up on the last day."*

Have you given your life entirely to Jesus? If so, then you are His son or daughter and have heard His voice. The fact that you have said "yes" to Jesus proves that He still speaks, and you can hear His voice.

John 12:32: *"And when I am lifted up from the earth, will draw all people to myself."*

God undoubtedly speaks through the scriptures. If you have picked up the Bible and spent considerable time reading it, you can be assured that God is speaking through it. Countless scriptures speak to the inspiration, truthfulness and importance of God's word. The writer of Hebrews says that the word of God is living and active.

Hebrews 4:12: *"For the word of God is living and active, sharper than any two-edged sword, piercing to the division of soul and of spirit, of joints and of marrow, and discerning the thoughts and intentions of the heart."*

As we read, study, meditate and pray through the scriptures, the words of God are living, active, speaking, revealing, convicting and piercing.

As you read the following scriptures, ask what the Holy Spirit is saying to you:

2 Timothy 3:16-17
2 Peter 1:20-21
Psalm 119
Romans 15:4
Romans 10:17
Joshua 1:8
Psalm 19:7-11

Another way that the Spirit of Jesus speaks to us is by bringing conviction of sin and righteousness.

John 16:7-11: *"Nevertheless, I tell you the truth: it is to your advantage that I go away, for if I do not go away, the Helper will not come to you. But if I go, I will send him to you. And when he comes, he will convict the world concerning sin and* *righteousness and judgment: concerning sin, because they do not believe in me; concerning righteousness, because I go to the Father, and you will see me no longer; concerning judgment, because the ruler of this world is judged."*

A few years ago, I was driving in my car, and I was about to exit onto the busiest highway in Calgary and out of nowhere, I was convicted of something I had done while working for a previous employer. To make a long story short, I hadn't been completely honest about a situation that had taken place while working there. The Spirit had been searching my inner man saying, "Randall, you need to make this right." Within a few days, I had contacted my previous boss and made things right."

Not only will the Holy Spirit convict us of the things we have done that don't please Him, but He will also convict us of the right thing to do in a situation. I once had my two young daughters with me, and we went to a store. While there, my youngest daughter grabbed something off the shelf and put it in her pocket. While loading the car, she said, "Daddy, look what I got." It was a cheap little toy worth $1.00. At that moment, I could have easily said, "We are already in the car, the employee won't care anyways, it's going to take me fifteen minutes to get the kids back into the store and back out to the car, etc." I knew the right thing to do was to go back into the store, speak to the employee and give it back. This might seem like a small and insignificant story, but the Lord cares deeply about the integrity of our hearts, and of our children's hearts.

God is still speaking to His people today! There is no doubt about it. He is still drawing all men to Himself. Where would we be without His voice?

Prayer:

Jesus, I thank you that you still speak today. You are a perfect leader, and you guide us in all that we do. I pray that you would open my ears to hear your voice.

Activation:

Grab your Bible and read through each of the scriptures below. Meditate on them and commit one or two to memory. Ask the Holy Spirit to speak to you through these scriptures. I suggest writing down what the Spirit is saying in your journal.

2 Timothy 3:16-17, 2 Peter 1:20-21, Psalm 119, Romans 15:4, Romans 10:17, Joshua 1:8, Psalm 19:7-11.

Ask the Holy Spirit if there is any wrong that needs to be made right in your life.

Chapter 4
God Speaks Through His Written Word

Those who live with an inner peace have built their lives on God's word. The only people who are successful at resisting lust, greed, and the temptations of the world are the ones who treasure the Word of God in their hearts. Jack Deere, former professor at Dallas Theological Seminary, suggests that these people are those who "have submitted themselves to and rooted themselves in the Word of God."[21]

The Scriptures are the standard for how God speaks to His people, and they must be the foundation of lives lived according to the voice of God. My friend and School of Biblical Studies Director serving with YWAM, Brian Hunsberger, says, "Wanting to hear from God and not reading your Bible is like waiting to receive a text from your friend, but you have your phone turned off." The scriptures are a lifeline to our spirits.

One of the most difficult seasons of our lives was the year my father-in-law passed away from pancreatic cancer. From diagnosis to his passing was less than five months. It's

---

[21] Jack Deere, Surprised by the Voice of God, (Grand Rapids, Michigan, Zondervan Publishing House, 1996) 103

difficult to describe the pain; so many unanswered questions. One day, while visiting him in the hospital, the family was chatting in the quiet room; the environment was heavy and sad. I noticed a Bible on one of the side tables in the room. I flipped it open and began silently reading the Psalms. Within thirty seconds, I could feel joy welling up inside of me. Joy? Amid pain, sadness, unknown. How? The word of God!

Some foundational verses speak to the fact that the Spirit of God inspires the written word, and is, therefore, spoken by God. As Paul writes a pastoral encouragement to Timothy, he states,

2 Timothy 3:16-17: *"All Scripture is breathed out by God and profitable for teaching, for reproof, for correction, and for training in righteousness, that the man of God may be complete, equipped for every good work."*

Most of us are familiar with Paul's words in 2 Timothy 3:16-17, but only a few of us know the two verses right before it. Paul writes a letter to his spiritual son Timothy and encourages him to continue being acquainted with the scriptures because they make you wise for salvation. The written word of God keeps us grounded; Paul knows it, and he makes sure that Timothy knows it too.

2 Timothy 3:14-15: *"But as for you, continue in what you have learned and have firmly believed, knowing from whom you learned it and how from childhood you have been acquainted with the sacred writings, which are able to make you wise for salvation through faith in Christ Jesus."*

The Apostle Peter points to the Holy Spirit as the source of the written word.

2 Peter 1:20: *"Knowing this, first of all, that no prophecy of Scripture comes from someone's own interpretation. For no prophecy was ever produced by the will of man, but men spoke from God as they were carried along by the Holy Spirit."*

We desperately need to be hungry for the word of God and a people who are rooted and grounded in its truth. My friend and mentor, Dr. Ron Smith once said "If you are not reading your Bible, you are not hungry enough."[22]

Listen to how the psalmist hungered for the word of God in Psalm 119.

Psalm 119:9-11: *"How can a young man keep his way pure? By guarding it according to your word. With my whole heart I seek you; let me not wander from your commandments! I have stored up your word in my heart, that I might not sin against you."*

Psalm 119:14: *"In the way of your testimonies I delight as much as in all riches."*

Psalm 119:16: *"I will delight in your statutes; I will not forget your word."*

Psalm 119:24: *"Your testimonies are my delight; they are my counselors."*

---

[22] Dr. Ron Smith, "Bible Meditation," (Lecture Notes, University of the Nations, January 2008)

Psalm 119:48: *"I will lift up my hands toward your commandments, which I love, and I will meditate on your statutes."*

Ron once encouraged a group of my friends to fast and pray for a hunger for God's word. I fasted for three days, wrote out the books of 1st, 2nd and 3rd John by hand, and prayed that God would make me hungry and ground me in His word. These days were foundational and set me on a path to have a love for the word of God. Paul states that the scriptures were written for our hope.

Romans 15:4: *"For whatever was written in former days was written for our instruction, that through endurance and through the encouragement of the Scriptures we might have hope."*

We live in a day and age where voices come at us from all angles. Social media, the news, politicians, podcasts, YouTube and the list continues. Hours and hours daily are spent on our phones, computers and television screens. I won't sit here and tell you it's all bad and that you can never use it again, but we need to be a people that are grounded in the word of God. We need the loudest voice in our head to be the rumblings of scripture. We will not survive this life if we are not planted and rooted in His word.

Do you desire to hear His voice? When the storms of life come do you want to be on the solid rock? Ask the Lord to make you a Psalm 1, man or woman, one who delights and meditates on the word day and night. The psalmist says this person will be like a tree planted by streams of water and yielding much fruit (Psalm 1:1-6).

The Power of the Written Word

During the Covid-19 pandemic, there was mass chaos, confusion, and many voices. If it wasn't politicians making a statement, it was doctors, and if the news wasn't commenting on it all, the ridiculousness that ensued on social media could put you in a spiral for days. I remember one day, I was in the middle of what turned out to be a four-hour-long Zoom call, and at one point, I had completely zoned out. I remember glancing over at my Bible, and feeling an intense hunger come over me to read the word of God. The Lord said to me, "If you are going to stay grounded in this time, you must meditate on my word." I remember getting off the Zoom call, grabbing my Bible, and meditating the word of God. It was like a refreshing waterfall was pouring over me.

Recently, Becky and I found ourselves waiting on the Lord for over a year as we felt like the Lord was transitioning us. We knew the transition was approaching, but we were waiting for His perfect timing and clarity. During this time, God used scripture to confirm and affirm this in our hearts. During this year of waiting, there was one week specifically where I read, heard or was given as an encouragement Isaiah 43:19 three separate times. Isn't it God's nature to confirm His word using the scripture? How beautiful is the faithfulness of God?

Dr. Ron Smith, founder of the School of Biblical Studies in Youth With a Mission, has written an excellent book on Bible meditation called "Hooked on the Word." I have listened to him teach many times on Bible meditation, and every time, I find myself excited to dive deep into the word. No other person in my life has influenced me more than Ron in Bible reading and meditation.

Here are ten ways in which Ron suggests diving into the Bible:[23]

1) Read the Bible out loud for 15 minutes every day.
2) Read the Bible out loud.
   Start with the shorter books (25 books of the Bible can be read in 30 minutes or less).
3) Read through the Bible quickly like a summer novel.
4) Read the Bible together with friends.
   While working with Youth With A Mission (YWAM), we took young adults overseas for two months at a time. Every time we went, we set aside a day and read through the entire New Testament; this usually took about thirteen hours. We would sit in a circle, taking turns reading.
5) Write out the Bible long-hand.
   This might seem crazy, but it was actually a command of the Lord for the King of Israel.
   Deuteronomy 17:18-20: *"And when he sits on the throne of his kingdom, he shall write for himself in a book a copy of this law, approved by the Levitical priests. And it shall be with him, and he shall read in it all the days of his life, that he may learn to fear the Lord his God by*

---

[23] Dr. Ron Smith, "Bible Meditation"

keeping all the words of this law and these statutes, and doing them, that his heart may not be lifted up above his brothers, and that he may not turn aside from the commandment, either to the right hand or to the left, so that he may continue long in his kingdom, he and his children, in Israel."

6) Listen to an audio Bible.
   Sometimes listening to an audio Bible is a great way to meditate on the word while you are out for a run or driving in your car or even falling asleep. We need to hear the word of the Lord so that it can build up our faith.
   Romans 10:17: *"So faith comes from hearing, and hearing through the word of Christ."*
7) Memorize the Bible.
   King David said in Psalm 63:3 that even in the night watches he meditated on the Lord.
8) Repetition of reading the Bible.
   Choose a book of the Bible and spend a month reading it. Take a verse and spend the next three days meditating on it.
9) Read through different translations of the Bible.
   For about 12 years, I read the English Standard Version of the Bible and still use it for study and preaching or teaching. In 2020, I read through the NLT version, and it was a breath of fresh air. I now use the NLT for my devotional reading.
   Try some of these versions: ESV, NLT, The Message, NKJV, NRSV.

10) Read the Bible out loud and then summarize each paragraph.

Do you want to hear God speak to you? Spend time reading the word. Start with fifteen minutes a day and then increase. Remember, this is not about checking off a box on a to-do list, this is not about reading through the Bible in a year (although that's not a bad idea), but this is about encountering Jesus in His word and allowing it to sink deep into your being. Sometimes, it seems God is not speaking, or you cannot hear Him clearly. During these times or seasons, I encourage you to dive deep into the written word of God. Feast on it; it will be nourishment for your spirit. Jesus is very clear that we cannot live on food alone.

Matthew 4:4: *"It is written, "'Man shall not live by bread alone, but by every word that comes from the mouth of God."*

The Illuminating Work of the Spirit

1 Corinthians 2:10-13: *"These things God has revealed to us through the Spirit. For the Spirit searches everything, even the depths of God. For who knows a person's thoughts except the spirit of that person, which is in him? So also no one comprehends the thoughts of God except the Spirit of God. Now we have received not the spirit of the world, but the Spirit who is from God, that we might understand the things freely given us by God. And we impart this in words not taught by human wisdom but taught by the Spirit, interpreting spiritual truths to those who are spiritual."*

The Holy Spirit is needed to bring to light the meaning of the scriptures. As we meditate and study God's word, the Holy Spirit reveals the truth about the word. This is, in part, what Jesus meant when He told His disciples about the role of the Holy Spirit.

John 16:13: *"When the Spirit of truth comes, he will guide you into all the truth, for he will not speak on his own authority, but whatever he hears he will speak, and he will declare to you the things that are to come."*

Our reading of the scripture should be bathed in prayer. Asking the Spirit to reveal the truth of what is being said, asking Him to reveal Jesus in the pages of the Bible. Some of our greatest encounters with the Lord should be in the pages of His word. Allow the words to wash over you and renew your mind.

Prayer:
God I thank you for Your word and that it will stand forever. I thank you that we have been granted all things that pertain to life and godliness, through the knowledge of your Son Jesus. Thank you that Your word reveals who you are and sustains us. I commit myself to your word as you say, "man cannot live on bread alone but every word that comes from the mouth of God."

Activation:

Meditate on and ask the Lord what He wants to speak to you through these verses: Ephesians 1, 3:14-20,
Psalm 1, 119, 139
1 Thessalonians 2:13
Acts 17:11

Chapter 5
Biblical Ways in Which God Speaks

God speaks in many different ways; He can talk to us however He chooses. He is so creative that He has created a whole spectrum of ways He communicates.

Proverbs 20:12: *"The hearing ear and the seeing eye, the Lord has made them both."*

As we explore the various ways God speaks, I want to echo the words of Darlene Cunningham, "Jesus is looking for listening hearts."[24] Are we open and expectant to hear God speak? Will our hearts be humble enough to receive how He desires to talk to us? Ultimately, God desires to speak to us not because we need answers to life's many questions, but because He wants to walk in a relationship with us. One reason why God is so creative in the way He speaks is so we don't make it into a formula of how He communicates with us. I find that in different seasons of my life, God speaks differently. Sometimes, He speaks loudly through dreams, sometimes through His written word, sometimes through His still small voice, and often through other people.

---

[24] Darlene Cunningham, Values Matter, 51

The first significant premise of hearing God's voice is a desire to hear from Him. During His ministry on earth, Jesus would often say, "he who has ears, let him hear." Meaning, do you want to hear? Do you desire to understand? Do you want to know what is on the heart of God for your future, your children, your friends, and your neighbour? Secondly, are you taking the time to listen to what He is saying? Our prayer life is usually one-sided; we have a list of things on our hearts, we bring the requests to God, and we pray, "*My* will on earth be done, as it is in *my* heart," and then finish. A relationship is a two way conversation. When I was in junior high and highschool I played in a jazz band. Our instructor would have us practice improvisation by doing an exercise called "call and response." One person would "call" by solo improvisation and the next person would "respond" by soloing back. This is how prayer should be. Sharing what is on our heart and then asking, "Lord, what is on your heart?" Asking for His insight into every situation. "God, is there anything you need to say to me about my relationships right now?" "Is there anything you want to tell me about my parenting? About my marriage?" I guarantee you there is something He wants to say about these specific areas and situations.

One night, I woke up from a dream. I don't remember the dream, but I will never forget what the Lord said, "Randall, if you keep disciplining your daughter in this manner, she will grow up to have a hard heart towards me." It put the fear of the Lord in me. I immediately told Becky the following day, and we agreed to find a new way to discipline our daughter. God is concerned with the way we parent our children. He is so faithful to teach us how to be good fathers and mothers.

Another time, I was driving home from the recycling depot. I was thinking about all the realities of being a young father. The Lord spoke so clearly to me, "Randall, the way you father Olivia is the way that she will understand who I am." The fear of the Lord came over me so strongly and I cried out to Him for grace and mercy. I so badly need His direction and leadership in being a father to our girls.

Let's dive into some of the biblical ways in which God speaks.

Promptings

Have you ever had an idea or thought come into your mind and you think, "Where did that come from?" Joy Dawson calls this "a nudge in our spirit that God wants to get our attention to do or say something."[25]

As we begin to recognize these promptings from the Lord, we will increasingly have them at work, school, the grocery store, or at any moment the Lord wants to get our attention. I encourage you to ask the Holy Spirit to increase His nudges in your life.

In high school, my family went camping one weekend in the summertime. While there, my older brother and I met some people and hung out with them a few times. At the end of our time together, I had a nudge in my spirit to share the good news of Jesus with them. I had no idea what I was doing. I was so nervous and ended up fumbling over my words as I tried to

---

[25] Joy Dawson, Forever Ruined For the Ordinary, 84

share with them about Jesus. They did not give their lives to Jesus at that moment, but I believe a seed was planted in their hearts. I can rest assured that I walked in obedience to His voice.

There have been other times when I have given into the fear of man and not been obedient to the nudging and promptings of the Holy Spirit. The more we yield to these promptings, the more they will come; obedience is key.

Repeated Thoughts

Maybe you have encountered a situation where you can't get someone off your mind (no, I'm not talking about that "special someone"). Sometimes, we are reminded of specific people in our lives over the course of a day or a week. I believe this is the Lord trying to get our attention. Maybe we are to pray for them or reconnect with them. I would encourage you to contact them and see how they are doing or ask the Lord, "God, you keep on bringing "John" to my mind. How can I partner with you in this?" My friend Matt said recently, "God interrupt whatever we are doing, so that we can join you in what you're doing." AMEN!

A few years ago, Becky and I worked with YWAM and we were required to raise our own funds. We had just had our first daughter and were living day-to-day. I remember getting a text one day from Becky saying, "We only have $7 left for groceries and gas this month; not sure what we are going to do." A couple of days later, we had a knock at our door. I opened the door, "Jason! How's it going? Come on in." We had not seen our friend Jason for quite some time. We talked briefly, and then he said, "Hey, I don't have long, but I can't get you guys off my mind; I felt like I was supposed to give you this." I looked down, and he handed me two Visa gift cards for $250 each! Praise the Lord! God is faithful and He provides for our needs.

We often overthink how God speaks to us. Too often, we think that God could only speak in a lightning bolt from heaven when, in fact, He is speaking right into our thought lives. As we go on this journey of hearing God's voice, we need to have our minds renewed so that we can learn and recognize the voice of God.

Romans 12:2: *"Do not be conformed to this world, but be transformed by the renewal of your mind, that by testing you may discern what is the will of God, what is good and acceptable and perfect."*

"Random" Thoughts or Situations

One of my favourite ways that God speaks to His people is through "random" thoughts or situations. There have been countless times when a thought will go through my head, but I know it is not from me, but has to have come from the Lord. I will share it in a particular setting, and it will bless the individual or group of people listening. There are also "random" situations that we find ourselves in, and the only explanation is that God was orchestrating it all along.

One of the things that Becky and I have learned over the years is to let the peace of God lead us in hearing His voice. If there is no peace, we don't move forward.

Roman 8:6: *"For to set the mind on the flesh is death, but to set the mind on the Spirit is life and peace."*
Colossians 3:15: *"And let the peace of Christ rule in your hearts, to which indeed you were called in one body. And be thankful."*

I would encourage you to entertain "random" God-honouring thoughts that come across your mind. You might be changing the trajectory of someone's life or even your own life. The apostle Paul gives us incredible advice regarding thoughts that go through our minds.

2 Corinthians 10:4-6: *"For the weapons of our warfare are not of the flesh but have divine power to destroy strongholds. We destroy arguments and every lofty opinion raised against the knowledge of God, and take every thought captive to obey Christ, being ready to punish every disobedience, when your obedience is complete."*

Music/Movies/Art

God is not limited by anything; He is both limitless and creative. I have friends who work in the Arts and Entertainment industry and believe that God is using them in a mighty way to speak to those around them and share the love of Jesus Christ with them.

Recently, I felt like the Lord asked me to watch a movie. I have a tough time sitting through movies or TV shows (just ask Becky), and this was a three-hour film; a classic nonetheless. Because I believe that the Lord had asked me to watch it, I was highly aware of every scene and every word in the script; I didn't want to miss anything. Because it was so long, I watched it over three days. Many scenes cut me to the heart. Scenes of betrayal, scenes of strong leadership, scenes of poor leadership, scenes of brokenness and of heartache. God taught me many things I will forever hold on to in those three hours.

Worship

Worship is one of the most significant catalysts for the Lord to speak. Have you ever been in a time of worship and felt like the Lord spoke to you, or you felt His presence? Maybe you had utterly unexplainable peace. The scriptures show us the power of worship.

2 Kings 3:15: *"But now bring me a musician." And when the musician played, the hand of the Lord came upon him."*

Worship is almost always a catalyst for the voice of God. I love to go for runs, and I will often listen to worship music, pray and commune with the Holy Spirit while I run. Usually, my mind will overflow with God's thoughts and dreams, and the Holy Spirit speaks to me about what He is asking me to step into. The next time you worship the Lord, listen to His voice. You will be surprised by what happens next.

Recently, our family was at an event with over 4000 people in attendance. We were all worshiping and praising the Lord. At one point, the leader invited everyone who wanted or needed a touch from God (or a filling of His Spirit) to come forward. We ran with a couple thousand others to the front. Our oldest daughter, Olivia (8) got on her knees, with arms raised in the air and began to weep and cry out to God. It was one of the most powerful moments I have ever been part of. On the drive home, I asked Olivia, "What was God doing at that moment?" With tears running down her face she said, "I was just experiencing the love of God and His presence." She continued to cry in the car for the next little while, continuing to encounter the heart of her heavenly Father.

Creation

Creation is forever speaking of who God is. The Bible speaks loudly to its reality.

Romans 1:20: *"For his invisible attributes, namely, his eternal power and divine nature, have been clearly perceived, ever since the creation of the world, in the things that have been made. So they are without excuse."*
Psalm 19:1-4: *"The heavens declare the glory of God, and the sky above proclaims his handiwork. Day to day pours out speech, and night to night reveals knowledge. There is no speech, nor are there words, whose voice is not heard. Their voice goes out through all the earth, and their words to the end of the world."*

There are many examples of God speaking in the Bible through His creation. Genesis 9:12-13 God speaks through the promise of the rainbow. I remember God speaking this truth to me when I was 18 years old. My parent's and I were driving home from the lake earlier than planned, because there was a storm. The storm ended while we were in the van, and a rainbow appeared. I remember God speaking so clearly to me that despite the fact that God's promise was to Noah thousands of years ago, the rainbow is still a promise from God to humanity today that He will not flood the earth again. At this point in my life, I didn't even know that God spoke.

God also spoke to the prophet Jeremiah through creation.

Jeremiah 1:11-12: *"And the word of the Lord came to me, saying, "Jeremiah, what do you see?" And I said, "I see an almond branch." Then the Lord said to me, "You have seen well, for I am watching over my word to perform it."*

In Jeremiah's interaction with God, God uses an almond branch to speak to Jeremiah, and then Jeremiah brings a message to the people of Israel.

Our family was on a trip recently, and we were out for a walk. I took this time to teach our girls, Olivia (8) and Gwen (6) that the Lord speaks to His people through creation. I told the girls to look around them; there was a lake, mountains, large trees, a sandy beach and many other things. Once they had looked around, I said "ask Jesus to highlight a part of His creation." Olivia picked the grass, and Gwen picked the lake. "Now, girls," I said, "ask the Lord what He wants to say to you through this part of His creation." Olivia said, "Just like each blade of grass is unique, so is each of the people He created (Psalm 139)." Did that just come from my eight-year-old's mouth? Wow! Gwen said, "I think God wants to say that He loves His creation (Genesis 1)." God speaks through His creation, even to our children!

<u>Spiritual Gifts</u>

Paul speaks of revelation outside of the Bible (<u>not</u> contrary to the Bible). I know this might scare some of you, but if we are going to be biblically based Christians, we must pay attention to all of scripture and not just the parts we are comfortable with.

Receiving revelation (hearing God speak) outside of the Bible comes in the form of spiritual gifts. 1 Corinthians 12 and 14 are the primary passages of scripture regarding spiritual gifts. Sandwiched in between these two chapters is the famous love chapter (1 Corinthians 13), which is often read at weddings, but actually has nothing to do with marriage. The context of 1 Corinthians 13 is revealed by the chapters on either side—spiritual gifts. Paul exhorts the believers to make love the aim concerning spiritual gifts. Can we be followers of Jesus who make love our aim in using the gifts of the Spirit? Can we stop trying to make ourselves look super spiritual? Our church once had a worship night where we spent a prolonged time worshiping and praising God. This particular night, which only included a few people, had a lady in attendance I had never seen before. When the night was over, she approached me and started talking with me; then proceeded to prophesy over everyone in attendance. While what she was sharing from the Lord was not wrong or harmful, the spirit in which she was operating seemed to be very self-focused; to make herself look spiritual. It seemed as though she wanted to validate who she was, instead of operating from a posture of love. This lady was completely new to our small city; she had no home church, had never attended our church, and was using the gifts of the spirit to make herself look good. This may seem judgemental, but you could tell by the way she spoke and delivered her words that it was more about her and less about building up the body. I thanked her for her encouraging words and then checked in with everyone in attendance if they were ok. This lady never returned to our church or future worship nights.

This is precisely why Paul writes to the "super spiritual" church in Corinth, to bring correction in how they operated in the gifts of the Spirit. Paul desires that they would make love their aim.

1 Corinthians 14:26: *"What then, brothers? When you come together, each one has a hymn, a lesson, a revelation, a tongue, or an interpretation. Let all things be done for building up."*

At the end of verse twenty-six, the last command is imperative: let all things be done to build up others. A revelation or message from the Lord to share with the gathered saints is not to make you or anybody else look good or "super spiritual," but to make much of Jesus, to yield to the working of the Holy Spirit, and to encourage the body. We will talk more about the gifts of the Spirit in the next chapter.

Dreams

The more I talk to others about the different ways that God speaks, the more I hear about others' dreams. It is fascinating to me how many people are having dreams that seem to have significance. Many of us are unaware that it could be God speaking to them. I love what Lou Engle says about dreams, "dreams are the last days language of the Holy Spirit."[26] He is referring to;

Joel 2:28-29: *"And it shall come to pass afterward, that I will pour out my Spirit on all flesh; your sons and your daughters shall prophesy, your old men shall dream dreams, and your young men shall see visions. Even on the male and female servants in those days I will pour out my Spirit."*

Lou says, "Why waste a third of our lives asleep without the language of heaven bombarding us?"[27]

Jack Deere in his book "Surprised by the Voice of God" states, "With the New Testament coming of the Holy Spirit, dreams, visions and other prophetic experiences become the normal experience for the whole church."[28] (Acts 2:17-18)

Dreams are the language of heaven; they can stay imprinted on our minds for the rest of our lives. Some dreams you undoubtedly know are from God. Other dreams must be prayed into and given insight from the Holy Spirit. In our home, every night before we go to bed, we pray for dreams from the Holy Spirit, that He would speak to us even while we sleep. God has spoken some incredible things to us. One night, when my oldest daughter Olivia was 4 or 5 years old, she had a dream from God. She woke up in the morning and said

---

[26] Lou Engle, "Lou Engle - Dreams and Visions - JESUS 16 Panel" Youtube Video, 11:43, March 19,2019, https://youtu.be/SG9RgdQhWT8?si=02NNffCGf5uDgNy9

[27] Lou Engle, "Lou Engle - Dreams and Visions - JESUS 16 Panel"

[28] Jack Deere, "Surprised by the Voice of God, 145

"Daddy, I had a dream last night of Jesus, and His eyes were like fire." Our young daughter had no grid for Jesus having eyes like fire. Jesus was revealing Himself to her while she was asleep.

Revelation 19:12-15: *"His eyes were as a flame of fire, and on his head were many crowns; and he had a name written, that no man knew, but he himself."*

When I was 17 or 18, I had a dream that I knew was not a "normal" dream. I still had no teaching in my life about God speaking or communicating with us in any way other than the Bible. In the dream, I was canoeing in the ditch to a neighbour's house, I then began walking towards the door and out of the front door came a witch (she wasn't dressed in black clothing with a black pointy hat; I just knew she was a witch). As she approached me, she was screaming at me in another language, and I started yelling back at her in tongues. I had no understanding of what this dream could mean. A few years later, I shared it with a friend, and they immediately said, "it sounds like some sort of spiritual warfare." There is a whole other realm that most believers never even think about, and in it there is a war going on.

God can speak to us in dreams for many reasons; here are a few:

1) Warfare
2) Direction
3) Comfort
4) Healing
5) Life Callings

Just as we need to test every prophetic word or voice we hear, we need to test our dreams. Some significant dreams in my life have brought an incredible amount of healing. On multiple occasions, I have dreamt of the Father heart of God, encountering His heart for me and weeping uncontrollably. These have brought incredible breakthroughs of healing in my life. Like I said, we pray for the Holy Spirit to speak to us in dreams every night because we desire to be bombarded by the language of heaven. Just recently, our youngest daughter Gwen (6) had a dream that Jesus came into her bedroom and began to play with her and Olivia and their cousins. This is exactly the heart of Jesus; meeting our children in their dreams and revealing His character (Matthew 18:1-5).

One morning, Becky woke up from a dream where she ran into a friend that she hadn't seen or talked to in awhile. It caught Becky's attention enough that she felt it would be good to reach out and connect with her later that day or even week. She then got up and got ready for the day, and got Olivia and Gwen ready to head to swimming lessons. As they pulled into the parking lot of the rec centre, Becky saw a vehicle that looked like the vehicle that the friend in the dream owned, and it reminded her of the dream. Immediately, she felt in her spirit that she would see her friend inside the rec centre, and said to God, "If this is you, you have my attention." After getting the girls ready for their swimming lesson, they walked out of the change room, and immediately saw her friend that she had just dreamed about! Gwen, Olivia, and Becky walked over and said hi, and Becky even shared that she knew she would see her that day, because of her dream! That day and into the week, Becky was able to connect with her, and listen to her as they were processing a difficult season of life. We can always trust that God is using these moments for His plans and purposes.

During a major life transition, I met with a few individuals from my church, letting them know I would be transitioning from my role. After the meeting ended, a few people left and a few stayed to continue chatting. One of the ladies who had already left, returned to the church a few minutes later and said, "Randall, can I chat with you for a bit?" She told me that six months before I made this announcement of our transition, she woke up from a dream on Christmas Eve, where Becky and I were transitioning out of our role and moving to a new city. From this dream, she knew that God was sharing with her that we would move on from our role at the church. This was incredibly encouraging! God is not a distant God, but is intricately involved in the details of our lives, and is indeed leading and guiding us.

I encourage you to ask the Lord to speak to you in dreams and visions. Every day, say, "Lord, speak to me in the night, in my dreams. I want to commune with your Spirit even while I sleep." I record all my dreams on an app on my phone. It is essential to keep track of your dreams, and to pray into their meaning over time if you need help understanding them.

Here are a few of the dreams found in the Bible:
Genesis 15:12-21 - Abraham's Dream
Genesis 28:21, 31:11 - Jacob's Dream
1 Kings 3:5 - Solomon's Dream
Genesis 37 - Joseph's Dream
Daniel 7:1 - Daniel's Dream
Acts 16:9-15 - Paul's Dream

Visions

The Bible tells us of God speaking through visions. Visions are not weird; they are common. They are one of the ways in which the Lord speaks to His people. There are an incredible amount of visions in the written word of God. The prophet, Joel speaks of a day when young men will see visions (Joel 2:28). In Acts 2, at the birth of the church, the words of Joel are fulfilled.

There are two types of visions, the first being a vision of the mind. The easiest way to think about this is your imagination. Take a moment, close your eyes and picture a purple elephant; this is your imagination, where God will often speak to us. Another way of saying this is, "God gave me a picture." I was in a time of worship once, and as soon as the music began, I had my eyes closed, and I saw a picture of a little girl running through a field of tall grass; the sun was shining, and she had a sundress on. Immediately, I began to weep as I felt the Lord showering His love and approval upon me. Scripture is filled with examples of dreams and visions.

Numbers 12:6: *"Hear my words: If there is a prophet among you, I the Lord make myself known to him in a vision; I speak with him in a dream."*

The second is similar; it is called an open vision or open-eyed vision. This is where your eyes are open, and a vision appears before you like a movie screen.

Acts 16:9-11: *"And a vision appeared to Paul in the night: a man of Macedonia was standing there, urging him and saying,*

"Come over to Macedonia and help us." 10 And when Paul had seen the vision, immediately we sought to go on into Macedonia, concluding that God had called us to preach the gospel to them."

I believe that visions are one of the most common ways the Lord speaks to His end-time church.

Here is a short list of visions in the Bible:
Genesis 15:1: *"After these things the word of the Lord came to Abram in a vision, saying, "Do not fear, Abram, I am a shield to you; Your reward shall be very great."*
Luke 1:5-23: *Zechariah has a vision of an angel.*
Acts 7:56: *"At the stoning of Stephen, the clouds are opened up, and Stephen has a vision of heaven and the Son of Man standing at the right hand of God."*
Acts 9: *"The Lord said to him in a vision, "Ananias." And he said, "Here I am, Lord." And the Lord said to him, "Rise and go to the street called Straight, and at the house of Judas look for a man of Tarsus named Saul, for behold, he is praying, and he has seen in a vision a man named Ananias come in and lay his hands on him so that he might regain his sight."*
Acts 10: *God gives Cornelius a vision.*
Acts 18:9-11: *God gives Paul a vision.*
2 Corinthians 12:1-11: *Paul has a vision and is caught up into heaven*
The Book of Revelation: *John has a vision and writes the entire book of Revelation.*

Audible Voice

In the Bible, God spoke in an audible voice many times; Moses talked to God face-to-face in Exodus 33:11, countless other times throughout the Old Testament, and the Father spoke audibly at the baptism of Jesus.

Matthew 3:13-17: *"And behold, a voice from heaven said, "This is my beloved Son, with whom I am well pleased."*

Another time, the Father spoke from heaven in an audible voice and some people thought it was thunder; others thought it was an angel from heaven.

John 12:27-30: *"Now is my soul troubled. And what shall I say? 'Father, save me from this hour'? But for this purpose I have come to this hour. Father, glorify your name." Then a voice came from heaven: "I have glorified it, and I will glorify it again." The crowd that stood there and heard it said that it had thundered. Others said, "An angel has spoken to him." Jesus answered, "This voice has come for your sake, not mine."*

On the mount of transfiguration, the audible voice of God is heard, again speaking to the identity of Jesus.

Luke 9:35: *"And a voice came out of the cloud, saying, "This is my Son, my Chosen One; listen to him!"*

When Paul was breathing out murderous threats he heard the audible voice of God.

Acts 9:4-6: *"And on his way to Damascus to kill more Christians, he fell off his horse, and the voice of God from heaven came, Saul, Saul, why are you persecuting me?"*

I personally have never heard the audible voice of God, but I have friends who have heard Him in this way. One day, a friend of mine was at the end of her shift at work. She got into her car and began to drive. As she got onto the highway, she heard the audible voice of God say, "quit your job." The next day, she gave her two-weeks notice, went on a mission trip with her church, and met a girl who lived in another city while she was there. Over the course of a week, they became friends and then became roommates. Within a couple of weeks, she got a job at a church in this new city, and the trajectory of her life completely changed. In the years following, she met her husband at this church and have now been married for many years.

Internal Audible Voice

Although I have never heard the audible voice of God with my physical ears, I have heard what some call the internal audible voice of God. The inner audible voice of God resounds so loud in your spirit you can almost hear it with your physical ears.

The Prophet Samuel as a child is an excellent example of the internal audible voice of God.

1 Samuel 3:7-10: *"Now Samuel did not yet know the Lord, and the word of the Lord had not yet been revealed to him. 8 And* *the Lord called Samuel again the third time. And he arose and went to Eli and said, "Here I am, for you called me." Then Eli perceived that the Lord was calling the boy. 9 Therefore Eli said to Samuel, "Go, lie down, and if he calls you, you shall say, 'Speak, Lord, for your servant hears.'" So Samuel went and lay down in his place. 10 And the Lord came and stood, calling as at other times, "Samuel! Samuel!" And Samuel said, "Speak, for your servant hears."*

The Prophet Ezekiel experiences the internal audible voice of God one day when the elders of Israel come to inquire of him.

Ezekiel 14:2-4: *"And the word of the Lord came to me: 3 "Son of man, these men have taken their idols into their hearts, and set the stumbling block of their iniquity before their faces. Should I indeed let myself be consulted by them? 4 Therefore speak to them and say to them, Thus says the Lord God: Any one of the house of Israel who takes his idols into his heart and sets the stumbling block of his iniquity before his face, and yet comes to the prophet, I the Lord will answer him as he comes with the multitude of his idols."*

As I was learning to hear God's voice, I sat down one morning to study and read a book about growing in this area. I was so excited! As I was in the motion of sitting down, the Lord spoke so loud it felt like an audible voice. He said, "You know you don't need to read another book on this to hear my voice; you just need to do it." Another time I heard the internal audible voice of God was when I was at a retreat with our church. At that time, I was dealing with shame about past decisions. We took a couple of hours in the afternoon during the retreat to listen to God's voice. Honestly, I was scared to take the time to listen, because I thought the Lord would condemn me because of my sin. I finally got the courage to take some time and listen to Him. I walked outside and found a big red chair in the middle of the retreat centre. The sun was shining down on it. I walked over to the chair, sat down and leaned back; as I leaned back, I closed my eyes and rested my head on the back of the chair. The sun was so warm. I couldn't have been sitting there for more than three seconds, when I heard a booming internal voice, "Randall, my son, with whom I am pleased." I had my Bible on my lap, and tears began streaming down my face. The Lord talked with me about some things in my life that needed to change, but He didn't start there, He began by showering His love, affection and pleasure over me. This moment has marked me.

The Still Small Voice

We often have grave misconceptions about what hearing God's voice sounds or looks like. We have this idea that if God speaks, there will be flashes of lightning and loud crackling thunder, and an audible voice comes booming from heaven. We miss hearing His voice so often because we have no idea what it sounds like. God is Spirit, and we have a spirit. The Lord communicates to us Spirit to spirit. This often sounds like a low whisper. This whisper often comes in the form of "God thoughts;" thoughts that go through our mind that would have never originated with us. When we are fixated on the loud voice or the flash of lightning, there is a good chance we will miss the voice of God. Elijah heard the still small voice of God.

1 Kings 19:11-13: *"And he said, "Go out and stand on the mount before the Lord." And behold, the Lord passed by, and a great and strong wind tore the mountains and broke in pieces the rocks before the Lord, but the Lord was not in the wind. And after the wind an earthquake, but the Lord was not in the earthquake. And after the earthquake a fire, but the Lord was not in the fire. And after the fire, the sound of a low whisper. And when Elijah heard it, he wrapped his face in his cloak and went out and stood at the entrance of the cave. And behold, there came a voice to him and said, "What are you doing here, Elijah?"*

As we grow with God, at times, it can seem as though His voice gets quieter. God will often speak in a whisper to draw us closer to His heart, because intimacy is the number one goal. The softer He speaks, the quieter we must get to hear Him. It requires us to quiet the noise in our lives, slow down and listen to Him. I can't help but think this is why the psalmist says, *"Be still and know that I am God"* (Psalm 46:10). The practice of waiting on God in silence is one that is often neglected; we must reawaken the call to quieting ourselves before Him.

One time, I was praying for a man, and as I listened to the Holy Spirit, I heard Him say, "Tell this man his family is going to be ok." Initially, I felt apprehensive, but I humbly submitted the word to him. As I shared the word with him, his eyes got big, and he said, "Just before you prayed for me, I was on a phone call with my family back home (in another country). My mother has just been admitted to the hospital, and they don't know what is wrong, and my family is concerned." Within minutes, this man went from being worried, to instead having the peace of God reign in his heart.

In Nehemiah we see a great example of God speaking in a whisper or a still, small voice.

Nehemiah 7:5: *"Then my God put it into my heart to assemble the nobles and the officials and the people to be enrolled by genealogy. And I found the book of the genealogy of those who came up at the first, and I found written in it."*

What a wonderful phrase, "My God put it into my heart." Sometimes, God speaks by laying things on our hearts. As a teenager, I asked my dad why he wanted to become a farmer. I recall him replying, "It was on my heart. I enjoyed it, and so I followed the thing in my heart." God will often speak to us by "putting it in our hearts." The still small voice often sounds like our thoughts, inner promptings, our conscience and the peace of God reigning.

Smith Wigglesworth said, "At the slightest whisper of his voice, I turn aside to obey."[29] The most important part of hearing His voice is that we obey.

The Holy Spirit is actively leading Paul on each of his missionary journeys throughout the known world. As we go through our lives, living surrendered to the Holy Spirit these

---

[29] Bethany Hicks, "Bethel School of the Prophets," (Lecture Notes, Redding, California, August, 2023)

verses should bring us great comfort. We should run to the Lord for His leading and direction.

Acts 20:22-23: *"And now, behold, I am going to Jerusalem, constrained by the Spirit, not knowing what will happen to me there, except that the Holy Spirit testifies to me in every city that imprisonment and afflictions await me."*

The Bible doesn't give us more detail about the "constraining of the Spirit." Was it a prophetic word? Was it a word of knowledge given to him by another individual? All we know is that the Spirit constrained him. He knew deep down that he had to go. I've heard it said, "You know it in your knower." Paul knew by the Holy Spirit that he had to go to Jerusalem; even though it would not go well when he went.

Memories

Shawn Bolz states, "Our brain is trained to remember natural things, but spiritual or supernatural memory comes out of his active voice."[30] One of the most incredible things the Holy Spirit does is bring to remembrance the things that Jesus taught and did.

John 14:26: *"But the Helper, the Holy Spirit, whom the Father will send in my name, he will teach you all things and bring to your remembrance all that I have said to you."*

---

[30] Shawn Bolz, Modern Prophets, (Studio City, CA: ICreate Productions, 2018) 93

This is one of the greatest tools of the Holy Spirit, bringing to remembrance the things of Jesus. The Holy Spirit will often remind me of prophetic words I have been given in the past or I will remember Bible verses that the Holy Spirit speaks to my heart. The direct command to remember is found hundreds of times in the scripture, even more if you take a variance of that command. Remembering what the Lord has done is imperative to walking a faith filled life. Isn't it wonderful that we have the Helper bringing to remembrance all that the Lord has done? I encourage you to ask the Holy Spirit to bring to remembrance the times you have seen the Lord work in your life. Meditate on the scriptures that recount the faithfulness of God to the Israelites. Reading the Psalms is a great place to start.

Objects

The Lord is creative, and the ways in which He speaks are endless, He even speaks through objects. In Jeremiah 1:13, God speaks to Jeremiah through a boiling pot. One day, I was sitting at my kitchen table, having my quiet time. My quiet times usually consist of reading the word, journaling, reading a book, prayer and worship. While I was sitting at the table reading the Bible, I looked up and saw a lamp. The phrase, *"Thy word is a lamp unto my feet, and I light unto my path"* (Psalm 119:105) flashed through my head. In a moment, the Lord spoke to me through the lamp in my living room to affirm that His word will light our path.

Through Other People

Many of us would agree that God has spoken to us through other people. God often speaks through others to bring direction, conviction, or encouragement. The Lord will often affirm or confirm a decision through others. Paul recounts in his letter to the Galatians when he had to bring correction to Peter.

Galatians 2:11-14: *"When Peter came to Antioch, I told him face to face that he was wrong. He used to eat with Gentile followers of the Lord until James sent some Jewish followers. Peter was afraid of the Jews and soon stopped eating with Gentiles. He and the others hid their true feelings so well that even Barnabas was fooled. But when I saw they were not really obeying the truth that is in the good news, I corrected Peter in front of everyone and said: Peter, you are a Jew, but you live like a Gentile. So, how can you force Gentiles to live like Jews?"*

When others come to us and feel like they may have a word of encouragement, direction, insight or even correction, we must take it to heart and lay it before the Lord. We must also walk with a great degree of humility; this is necessary when receiving a word of caution, warning or correction. Walking in pride is when we put up walls and don't allow others to speak into our lives. We all have blind spots or areas of our lives that still need sanctification and the work of the Holy Spirit. We also all see life through certain lenses and our lenses don't see the full picture all the time.

Another way that God speaks through people is the affirmation of a gift or life calling. When those around us affirm and confirm over and over something that is on our hearts, we can trust that the Lord is speaking through them into that area in our lives. I will be forever indebted to those who affirmed me in leading worship. I remember the first time I led a worship song in front of a church; my neighbour was the sound tech at his church, and he asked if I wanted to lead a song for the offering time. I was so nervous. I am so grateful that I had people who saw something in me and encouraged me in it.

Angels

One of the most common ways God spoke in the scriptures was through angels. The Bible is very clear that angels are not to be worshiped; Jesus is the only one worthy of worship.

Hebrews 1:13-14: *"And to which of the angels has he ever said, "Sit at my right hand until I make your enemies a footstool for your feet"? Are they not all ministering spirits sent out to serve for the sake of those who are to inherit salvation?"*

Angels are ministering spirits sent out to serve those who will inherit salvation. If you are a follower of Jesus Christ and believe in Him, you probably have been ministered to by an angel, even if you don't know it.

Hebrews 13:2: *"Do not neglect to show hospitality to strangers, for thereby some have entertained angels unaware."*

Psalm 91:11: *"For he will command his angels concerning you to guard you in all your ways."*

In Acts, Philip receives direction from the Lord:

Acts 8:26: *"Now an angel of the Lord said to Philip, "Rise and go toward the south to the road that goes down from Jerusalem to Gaza." This is a desert place."*

Every Christmas we read the Christmas story in Luke and angels play a key role in leading different people. Mary and Joseph, Zechariah and even the shepherds in the fields. In the first chapter of Luke we see several accounts of angels as messengers from God. In the second chapter of Luke the shepherds are met by a whole host of angels.

Luke 2:8-11: *"And in the same region there were shepherds out in the field, keeping watch over their flock by night. And an angel of the Lord appeared to them, and the glory of the Lord shone around them, and they were filled with great fear. And the angel said to them, "Fear not, for behold, I bring you good news of great joy that will be for all the people. For unto you is born this day in the city of David a Savior, who is Christ the Lord."*

The book of Acts records many testimonies of angels speaking to people in dreams or visions. Acts 1:10-11, 5:18-20, 7, 8:26, 10.

Testimonies

Joy Dawson states that "statistics prove that more people are brought to faith in Christ and discipled through one-on-one personal testimony than any other way."[31] Have you ever heard someone share a testimony of God working in their life, and it impacts you greatly? Maybe you are believing for God to bring a breakthrough in your life, and someone shares a story where they saw God move miraculously, and it speaks to you. The apostle Peter becomes a disciple of Jesus because of the testimony of his brother Andrew. This is a big deal!

John 1:40-42: *"One of the two who heard John speak and followed Jesus was Andrew, Simon Peter's brother. He first found his own brother Simon and said to him, "We have found the Messiah" (which means Christ). He brought him to Jesus. Jesus looked at him and said, "You are Simon the son of John. You shall be called Cephas" (which means Peter)."*

Countless people throughout history have given their lives to Jesus and heard Him speak to them through the power of testimony. Revelation 19:10 states, *"For the testimony of Jesus is the spirit of prophecy."* What does this mean? It means that sharing what God is doing in our lives gives others hope and speaks into their situation what God desires to do for them. Every time we give a testimony of what God has done in our lives we open up the door for God to work in someone else's life in a similar fashion. This should encourage us to share our stories of how God is working in our lives with others.

---

[31] Joy Dawson, Forever Ruined for the Ordinary, 81

My older brother has been dealing with chronic pain for many years. From not being able to work, to countless appointments with doctors and specialists, it has radically altered his life and the life of his family. Despite the constant pain that my brother endures, he has committed to God that he would not allow it to negatively impact his relationship with Him. This testimony is an example of allowing the Lord to speak to others through our experiences. I have been extremely challenged by my brother's journey to not allow the struggles I face to hinder my relationship with the Lord.

Children

Becky and I aim to cultivate a culture of listening to what Jesus wants to say in our home. Whether it is as we put our kids to bed, at the kitchen table while eating a meal or even on family walks, our desire is to teach our girls to hear God speak. Some of the most profound things have come from our children's mouths as we listen to the Spirit of Jesus!

Matthew 11:25-26: *"At that time Jesus declared, "I thank you, Father, Lord of heaven and earth, that you have hidden these things from the wise and understanding and revealed them to little children; yes, Father, for such was your gracious will."*

Yes, God speaks to children, our girls hear Him all the time. I've heard it said countless times, "There is no junior Holy Spirit." The same Holy Spirit is speaking to all of us. Children will often hear the Lord's voice louder and clearer than adults, because adults have years of doubts, blinders and hindrances that we must wade through.

One day after school, Olivia wanted to draw. She asked Becky, "Mommy, what should I draw?" Becky replied, "Why don't you ask the Holy Spirit for a picture?" Olivia reluctantly agreed. After quite some time, Becky had completely forgotten about the situation, as she had a few things to do around the house. Olivia came and showed her the picture she had drawn, and in amazement Becky knew it was a drawing of the Calgary Tower, and asked, "Did the Holy Spirit speak anything to you about this picture?" Olivia shared that she felt the Lord was leading our family to move to Calgary. We were in a season of waiting on God's direction, and the Lord used this as one of many confirmations in our decision.

One of my greatest joys is to see my girls learn to recognize and learn to hear God's voice. I hope and pray that they will always know and listen to Him. We are to train our children in the ways of God.

Deuteronomy 4:9: "Only take care, and keep your soul diligently, lest you forget the things that your eyes have seen, and lest they depart from your heart all the days of your life. Make them known to your children and your children's children."

I want to encourage you as you learn to recognize the voice of God in your life and take your children on the journey. Teach them that God speaks in many different ways. Encourage them to listen to the Lord throughout their day, maybe at school or the playground. **<u>Appropriately</u>** invite them into some of the decisions you and your spouse need to make. Encourage them to listen to God for others (prophecy). I guarantee you, it will not only impact their world, but yours too!

One of the enemy's greatest tactics is fear. He uses it in the lives of adults and children alike. Every now and then, our girls will have scary dreams; we use this as a time to point them to Jesus. Get your child to listen to Jesus in the middle of the night. Get them to ask where Jesus is in their room or what Jesus wants to say to them at that moment. Jesus will show up and destroy every ounce of fear. One night Olivia woke me up because our youngest daughter, Gwen, had a scary dream. I went to their room and Gwen was crying in her bed. Through her tears she said, "Daddy, sing that worship song." I had no idea what song she was talking about, but I began to worship and the presence of Jesus entered the room, and as a result, all fear left!

God is so creative! This is not an exhaustive list of how God speaks, He speaks in many different ways. As you think through all the ways in which He speaks, you will begin to realize that you hear Him more than you might have previously recognized, and that He is speaking all the time.

Prayer:
Jesus, I praise you and thank you for being such a creative God. Thank you for speaking to your children in so many different ways. I ask that you begin to speak to me in new ways I never knew existed. Help me be attentive to your voice.

Activation:

Try these exercises to engage in hearing God speak:

1) Pick an object from your surroundings, and ask, "Lord, what do you want to say to me?"

2) Close your eyes and ask the Lord for a picture, and ask "Lord, what do you want to say to me from this picture?"

3) Pick a friend or family member. Ask the Lord for a word or picture to give to them. If you get a picture, ask the Holy Spirit what the picture means and if He wants you to share it with your friend or family member.

4) If you have children, begin to teach them that Jesus speaks. Get them to start asking Him these questions as well.

5) Journaling Prayer: Ask the Holy Spirit specific questions and journal His response.
      a) What do you want to say to me right now?
      b) How can I grow in my relationship with my spouse?
      c) How can I grow in my parenting?
      d) How do you feel about me right now?
      e) Is there anything that is grieving your heart?

Chapter 6
Spiritual Gifts

God has poured out His Spirit and has given spiritual gifts to His church.

Joel 2:28-29: *"And it shall come to pass afterward, that I will pour out my Spirit on all flesh; your sons and your daughters shall prophesy, your old men shall dream dreams, and your young men shall see visions. Even on the male and female servants in those days, I will pour out my Spirit."*

According to Acts 2, Joel's prophecy is fulfilled, and the Holy Spirit is poured out. The apostles and many others were in the upper room waiting upon the Lord. As they were waiting, a mighty rushing wind came, the Holy Spirit was poured out, and tongues of fire were upon their heads, and they began to prophesy. Not only do we see the beginning of the church, but also the ability for all believers to be empowered by the Holy Spirit for righteous living and to do the works of Jesus, and for boldness to share the gospel and operate in the gifts of the Spirit.

These gifts are listed in Romans 12 and 1 Corinthians 12. They are considered gifts of grace, as the Holy Spirit empowers individuals to operate in them. Romans 12:3-8 lists seven gifts: prophecy, serving, teaching, exhortation, giving, leadership and mercy. While 1 Corinthians 12 gives a list of nine gifts: word of wisdom, word of knowledge, faith, gifts of healing, miracles, prophecy, distinguishing between spirits, tongues, and interpretation of tongues.

    The gifts of the Spirit are just that; gifts. They are received by grace, and they are released in our lives through faith. They do not make anyone more holy or more spiritual. There is nothing we can do to earn them, but there are ways in which we can walk in them with greater capacity if we steward them well. The parable of the talents is not in the context of spiritual gifts, but the principle of stewardship is directly relatable (Matthew 25:14-30). The main thrust of the parable is to be faithful with what you have been given. If you have been faithful with little, you will be given more. The Lord will give us more as we eagerly desire and walk in the spiritual gifts. Shawn Bolz says, "Think of God's gifts more like a partnership than a lottery; if you actively desire to partner with God and desire to bring about his kingdom on earth, then how could he say no? He actually wants it more than you do."[32]

    Praise the Lord, that the Father sent the gift of the Holy Spirit. He is the comforter, the sustainer, the Helper, the Spirit of wisdom and revelation, and the Spirit of truth and life. He is also the gift giver and has gifts for the church. I am blessed and privileged to have two daughters. One of the things that I do with them is take them on daddy/daughter dates regularly. I love spending time with them and getting to know who they

---

[32] Shawn Bolz, Modern Prophets, 101

are as they mature and grow into who God has called them to be. From time-to-time, if it has been awhile since our last date, they beg me to take them out. They know that when we go on a date, there are often, if not always, treats involved. Sometimes, even a gift. I can't help but think of Paul's admonition in 1 Corinthians 14:1 to *"earnestly desire spiritual gifts."* Paul wants the church to be zealous after the gifts of the Spirit, because he knows how important they are to the church and their health. It must grieve the Spirit of God when we do not eagerly desire His gifts. How weird is it that the church pushes the gifts of the Spirit to the side? Many in the church today don't like this verse and eagerly skip over it, or they don't read it slowly enough to realize what it is saying. EAGERLY DESIRE spiritual gifts. They emphasize the first part, "pursue love," but not the rest of the verse. Let's be a people who are zealous after the gifts of the Spirit!

    We must lay some groundwork before moving onto the point I want to make. Paul starts by commanding the church to pursue love. If we want the context for love, we must read 1 Corinthians 13. As previously said, 1 Corinthians 13 has nothing to do with marriage; it is in the context of spiritual gifts. Instead of loving one another by using the Spiritual gifts to build up the body of Christ, the Corinthians were using the gifts of the Spirit to try and make themselves look spiritual. Paul brings a correction and commands them to use the gifts in love.

1 Corinthians 13: *"If I speak in the tongues of men and of angels, but have not love, I am a noisy gong or a clanging cymbal. And if I have prophetic powers, and understand all* *mysteries and all knowledge, and if I have all faith, so as to remove mountains, but have not love, I am nothing. If I give away all I have, and if I deliver up my body to be burned, but have not love, I gain nothing. Love is patient and kind; love does not envy or boast; it is not arrogant or rude. It does not insist on its own way; it is not irritable or resentful; it does not rejoice at wrongdoing, but rejoices with the truth. Love bears all things, believes all things, hopes all things, endures all things. Love never ends. As for prophecies, they will pass away; as for tongues, they will cease; as for knowledge, it will pass away. For we know in part and we prophesy in part, but when the perfect comes, the partial will pass away. When I was a child, I spoke like a child, I thought like a child, I reasoned like a child. When I became a man, I gave up childish ways. For now we see in a mirror dimly, but then face to face. Now I know in part; then I shall know fully, even as I have been fully known. So now faith, hope, and love abide, these three; but the greatest of these is love."*

Paul gives a clarion call to love; be patient, kind, don't boast, don't envy, don't be arrogant or rude. He implores the Corinthians to continue using their gifts, but lovingly use them to build up the Church. By using the gifts we have been given by the Spirit in the proper manner, we are actually walking in love. Let's take a closer look at some of the gifts to see how God uses them to communicate to His people.

We all have the ability to walk in every spiritual gift. If we all have the Holy Spirit in us, and He is the one who gives the gifts, then we can potentially operate in all the gifts.

1 Corinthians 12:11: *"All these are empowered by one and the same Spirit, who apportions to each one individually as he wills."*

At the right time, in the right place, and situation, if we are walking in step with the Spirit, He can release certain gifts through us as He desires. This means that we may walk in different gifts at different times because of what the Lord desires to do in a certain setting. Our job is to walk yielded to Him so He can use us however He wants.

Gifts Related to Hearing God

1 Corinthians 12:8-11: *"For to one is given through the Spirit the <u>utterance of wisdom</u>, and to another the <u>utterance of knowledge</u> according to the same Spirit, to another faith by the same Spirit, to another gifts of healing by the one Spirit, to another the working of miracles, to another <u>prophecy</u>, to another the <u>ability to distinguish between spirits</u>, to another <u>various kinds of tongues</u>, to another the <u>interpretation of tongues</u>. All these are empowered by one and the same Spirit, who apportions to each one individually as he wills."*

Six of the nine gifts found in 1 Corinthians are related to God speaking. These gifts allow believers to see, understand and know a part of the Lord's heart and perspective for themselves and others. These gifts are the word of wisdom, the word of knowledge, the gift of prophecy, and the discerning of spirits, tongues, and interpretation of tongues. Let's dive into each one and look at biblical examples of their use.

Word of Wisdom - 1 Corinthians 12:8

A word of wisdom is when the Spirit of God empowers you with divine wisdom in a situation; dealing with a matter and applying knowledge and facts. This isn't wisdom that comes with age and life experience; although this is beneficial, and God uses this, this wisdom is from His Spirit—heavenly solutions to earthly problems. With this gift, we become Spirit-empowered kingdom problem solvers.

King Solomon was the wisest person ever to live. He went to the Lord and asked for wisdom; we read about it in 1 Kings 3:3-15. It pleased the Lord that Solomon asked for wisdom and understanding. King Solomon was given divine wisdom, and people from all over the world came to see him. The Queen of Sheba visited Solomon because of his great wisdom and wealth. You can read about this in 1 Kings 10. We also see King Solomon operating in this in 1 Kings 3:16-28. Two women who are in a dispute about whose child had died come to him. Solomon was given the wisdom to bring a heavenly solution to the problem. We need the Spirit of wisdom more than ever in today's society. There are countless earthly problems just waiting for kingdom solutions through the gift of wisdom. In the story of Joseph (Genesis 37-50), we see Pharaoh talking to his servants about Joseph saying, *"Can we find a man like this, in whom is the Spirit of God?"* Joseph was solving earthly problems with kingdom solutions. What if the world began to look to the church for its solutions?

God has words of wisdom that are just waiting to be released for His kingdom purposes; in your workplaces, in your schools, in your homes and in your churches. Those of you who are police, doctors, nurses, firefighters and EMS, what if you were clothed with supernatural wisdom?

Word of Knowledge - 1 Corinthians 12:8

A word of knowledge is when the Holy Spirit reveals knowledge about a situation that could not be known by any human means. Elizabeth receives a word of knowledge about who Mary is carrying (The Messiah), because her baby (John the Baptist) kicked inside of her.

Luke 1:41-44: *"And when Elizabeth heard the greeting of Mary, the baby leaped in her womb. And Elizabeth was filled with the Holy Spirit, and she exclaimed with a loud cry, "Blessed are you among women, and blessed is the fruit of your womb! And why is this granted to me that the mother of my Lord should come to me? For behold, when the sound of your greeting came to my ears, the baby in my womb leaped for joy."*

Jesus receives a word of knowledge about Nathanael, causing Nathanael to believe in Jesus. Jesus knows about Nathaniel's character and history before ever meeting him.

John 1:47-50: *"Jesus saw Nathanael coming toward him and said of him, "Behold, an Israelite indeed, in whom there is no deceit!" Nathanael said to him, "How do you know me?" Jesus answered him, "Before Philip called you, when you were under the fig tree, I saw you." Nathanael answered him, "Rabbi, you are the Son of God! You are the King of Israel!" Jesus answered him, "Because I said to you, 'I saw you under* *the fig tree,' do you believe? You will see greater things than these."*

We see in Acts 5 that Peter is given supernatural knowledge about Ananias and Sapphira lying to him about the sale of their property (read Acts 5:1-11).

I have seen many operating in the gift of the word of knowledge. A word of knowledge can also come through experiencing a "random" pain in your body that you have never had before. This could indicate that God wants to heal some in your midst. If you have pain in your shoulder, it could be that God desires to heal someone of a dislocated shoulder or chronic shoulder pain. One time, I was sitting at the back of the sanctuary of a church. It was a stressful season of life and the stress was manifesting in my body as jaw pain. At the end of the church service the preacher began to pray, as he was praying he pointed straight at me and said you are being healed of jaw pain. My stomach sank, because the pain was completely gone. The ironic part of the story was that this happened a week later in a completely different church. The Lord was trying to get my attention so that the worry and stress that I was carrying could be released to Him. A word of knowledge can also come from a "random" thought about someone's life. Scripture is filled with examples of this gift. I encourage you to read these for yourselves: 1 Samuel 9-10, 1 Kings 14:2-3, 2 Kings 5:20-27, 6:8-12, John 4:18-29, Matt 9:4, Acts 10:19.

Dan McCollam, author, speaker and prophetic trainer refers to the word of knowledge as "prophecies twin sister."[33] Prophecy is hearing from God and speaking into someone's future, while a word of knowledge is hearing from God about someone's past or present. While serving with Youth With A Mission, we would activate the word of knowledge through what we called "treasure hunts." We would ask the Holy Spirit to show us someone and something about someone's life and then go and find them, either in a mall, store, gas station or somewhere around the city. Seeing God work this way and how faithful He speaks to our hearts was incredible!

On one occasion, I was with a few others; we prayed and asked the Holy Spirit what He wanted to do. I received a picture of an elderly lady wearing a red jacket. We went to a few places and found no one meeting this description. After an hour of looking, we entered a coffee shop, grabbed some coffee and food, and sat down. As we sat down, I spotted an elderly lady with a red jacket on, and she was sitting with what looked like her daughter and granddaughter. I knew right away we needed to go over and talk with her. After a while, myself and another gentleman in our group walked over and engaged in conversation with her. At first, she seemed very uncomfortable, but as we spoke, she warmed up. I shared with her our story about how we prayed and God showed us who we should talk to. I said, "God wants you to know that He has not forgotten you and you are not alone." Her eyes began to well up with

---

[33] Dan McCollam, Basic Training for Prophetic Activation. (Vacaville, California: iWAR and SOUNDS OF THE NATIONS, 2012) 81

tears as she listened to us share the things that were on the heart of God for her.

These moments have the potential to change the trajectory of someone's life. When people encounter a living God, a healthy disorientation comes. They begin to ask different questions: who am I, why am I here, and is God real? People are desperately hungry to encounter God; they just don't know it!

Prophecy

1 Corinthians 14:3: *"The one who prophesies speaks to people for their upbuilding and encouragement and consolation."*

In its simplest form, prophecy is hearing God for others and speaking it. Prophecy is a Holy Spirit inspired word for upbuilding, encouragement and comfort. This has many forms. It can come in the form of preaching the word of God, getting a sense in prayer that God wants to do a specific thing in someone's life, receiving a picture for someone, etc. Preaching the word of God is one of the most significant and common forms of prophecy. Because the Bible is the written word of God, when pastors preach, there is an element of prophecy, granted they are being true to what the scriptures say. There have been times when I have preached a message, and people have come to me saying your preaching has confirmed the decision I need to make. This puts the fear of God in me, and should put the fear of God in all those who desire to preach God's word.

In his book Basic Training in the Prophetic, Kris Vallotton states that prophecy has two primary components;

foretelling and forthtelling.[34] Foretelling is to tell of future events like the prophet Agabus.

Acts 11:28: *"And one of them named Agabus stood up and foretold by the Spirit that there would be a great famine over all the world (this took place in the days of Claudius)."*

Forthtelling, on the other hand, is to cause the future. An example of this is Ezekiel prophesying to the dry bones.

Ezekiel 37:1-10: *"The hand of the Lord was upon me, and he brought me out in the Spirit of the Lord and set me down in the middle of the valley; it was full of bones. And he led me around among them, and behold, there were very many on the surface of the valley, and behold, they were very dry. And he said to me, "Son of man, can these bones live?" And I answered, "O Lord God, you know." Then he said to me, "Prophesy over these bones, and say to them, O dry bones, hear the word of the Lord. Thus says the Lord God to these bones: Behold, I will cause breath to enter you, and you shall live. And I will lay sinews upon you, and will cause flesh to come upon you, and cover you with skin, and put breath in you, and you shall live, and you shall know that I am the Lord." So I prophesied as I was commanded. And as I prophesied, there was a sound, and behold, a rattling, and the bones came together, bone to its bone. And I looked, and behold, there were sinews on them, and flesh had come upon them, and skin had covered them. But*

---

[34] Kris Vallotton, Basic Training For the Prophetic Ministry. (Shippensburg, PA: Destiny Image Publishers) 42

there was no breath in them. Then he said to me, "Prophesy to the breath; prophesy, son of man, and say to the breath, Thus says the Lord God: Come from the four winds, O breath, and breathe on these slain, that they may live." So I prophesied as he commanded me, and the breath came into them, and they lived and stood on their feet, an exceedingly great army."

I was in a prayer meeting once, and we were praying for one another. Before this meeting, my wife and I believed God was calling us to make a significant life transition and would require a giant step of faith into the unknown. We were waiting for the right time. During the meeting, a man from our church said to me, "Randall, I believe this year you will run with reckless abandonment in your faith, like in your younger years." I wrote this word down in my notes app on my phone and forgot about it. Seven months later, we stepped out into the great unknown, believing that the Lord was asking us to take a risk. One day, I was scrolling through my phone and came across this word. It provided incredible encouragement and comfort, knowing that the Lord had spoken!

Prophecy can profoundly affect the lives of those who receive it. I would not be where I am today without the gift of prophecy continually calling me forward. So many have spoken into my life and confirmed and affirmed what God is calling me to. The body of Christ is not walking in all its potential because many do not walk in the gift of prophecy.

Paul speaks of the deep things (or desires) of our hearts being revealed through the gift of prophecy.

1 Corinthians 14:24-25: *"But if all prophesy, and an unbeliever or outsider enters, he is convicted by all, he is called to account by all, 25 the secrets of his heart are disclosed, and so, falling on his face, he will worship God and declare that God is really among you."*

Prophecy reveals the things in our hearts that only we and God know about, calling them forth into being, the desires that some of us have never told anyone because we are too afraid that we cannot accomplish them.

Paul implores each one of us to pursue the gift of prophecy.

1 Corinthians 14:1: *"Pursue love, and earnestly desire the spiritual gifts, especially that you may prophesy."*

Who is the gift of prophecy for? Every single believer. Every believer can prophesy! If it wasn't for the entire church, Paul wouldn't tell them to pursue prophecy.

1 Corinthians 14:31: *"For you can all prophesy one by one, so that all may learn and all be encouraged."*

Discernment

I say this with great conviction: we live in a day and age where the body of Christ needs the gift of discernment more than ever before. "Discernment is the God-given or Spirit-empowered ability to understand the spirit motivating a person or event."[35] Hebrews 5:14 says that we need to use senses to discern between good and evil. We need discernment when we are raising our kids, we need discernment in our places of work, we need discernment in our churches and friendships. Paul states the importance of discernment in his letter to the Ephesian church.

Ephesians 5:6-10: *"Let no one deceive you with empty words, for because of these things the wrath of God comes upon the sons of disobedience. Therefore do not become partners with them; for at one time you were darkness, but now you are light in the Lord. Walk as children of light (for the fruit of light is found in all that is good and right and true), and try to discern what is pleasing to the Lord."*

When someone is operating in the gift of discernment, they will often get a sense of the situation. This can happen through a turning stomach about a problem or something spoken. I know people who will even get such an upset stomach that they want to vomit if an evil spirit is present. In these moments, it is an opportunity to press into the Holy Spirit and ask, "Holy Spirit, what are you doing? What do you want to say? How can I partner with you?"

One downfall with discernment is that someone immature in this gift will begin to judge a situation or person, rather than press into what the Holy Spirit wants to say or do. I believe that the main reason God gives us the gift of

---

[35] Dr. Bill Hamon, 70 Reasons for Speaking in Tongues (Stafford, Virginia: Parsons Publishing House, 2010) 119

discernment is to intercede and tear down the enemy's plans. We must remember in all situations that our battle is not against flesh and blood.

Ephesians 6:12: *"For we do not wrestle against flesh and blood, but against the rulers, against the authorities, against the cosmic powers over this present darkness, against the spiritual forces of evil in the heavenly places."*

When operating in discernment, we must immediately take it to the Lord and ask Him what we are to do.

Tongues
There are three types of tongues found in the Bible:
1) Personal Prayer Language
The personal prayer language is for all who are believers filled with the Holy Spirit. Paul says the one who speaks in a personal prayer language is speaking mysteries to God in the Spirit, and it is for personal edification. It should be done in private, or in a space where all believers have an understanding that they are praying in a personal prayer language and no interpretation is needed. Paul also states that he thanks God he prays in tongues more than all (1 Corinthians 14:18).

1 Corinthians 14:2: *"For one who speaks in a tongue speaks not to men but to God; for no one understands him, but he utters mysteries in the Spirit."*
1 Corinthians 14:4: *"The one who speaks in a tongue builds up himself, but the one who prophesies builds up the church."*

1 Corinthians 14:14-15: *"For if I pray in a tongue, my spirit prays but my mind is unfruitful. What am I to do? I will pray with my spirit, but I will pray with my mind also; I will sing praise with my spirit, but I will sing with my mind also."*
1 Corinthians 14:18: *"I thank God that I speak in tongues more than all of you."*

If you have not received your personal prayer language, I implore you to ask the Father for it; receive it and exercise it by faith. Ask those who you know possess the gift and get them to lay hands on you and pray for you.

Matthew 7:7-11: *"Ask and it will be given to you; seek and you will find; knock and the door will be opened to you. For everyone who asks receives; the one who seeks finds; and to the one who knocks, the door will be opened. "Which of you, if your son asks for bread, will give him a stone? Or if he asks for a fish, will give him a snake? If you, then, though you are evil, know how to give good gifts to your children, how much more will your Father in heaven give good gifts to those who ask him!"*

As you spend time praying in tongues, the Holy Spirit will often speak to you. It will often come in the form of gentle whispers, while other times it may sound like a shout from the mountain tops!

2) Earthly Language not Formally Known to the Speaker (Acts 2)

The Holy Spirit is so creative and works in incredible ways. One of the ways He moves through His church is by empowering them to speak in a language not formerly known to them. There are many stories in church history where missionaries have spoken in a language they do not know for the sake of sharing the gospel.

Eddie L. Hyatt shares a few stories on this type of tongue in his book 2000 years of Charismatic Christianity. "In 1170-1221, Dominic, a contemporary of Francis of Assisi, began a preaching order known as the Dominicans. On a journey through Europe, Dominic and his companions joined a group of Germans, traveled with them for a time and received their hospitality. Because Dominic did not understand their language, he could not talk to them. On their fourth day together, Dominic reproached himself for being so unconcerned with the eternal needs of his fellow travelers and suggested to his companion that they "kneel down and pray to God that he would teach us the language for we are not able to announce to them the Lord Jesus". God answered their prayer enabling them to speak to the Germans in their language. Astonished at Dominic's ability to suddenly speak their language, the Germans listened intently over a four day period as Dominic shared the Gospel."[36]

---

[36] Eddie L. Hyatt, 2000 Years of Charismatic Christianity (Lake Mary, Florida: Charisma House, 2002) 60

"Francis Xavier lived from 1506-1552. In his missions to the far east, he is said to have spoken Japanese "as if he had lived in Japan all his life". When the time came for his canonization by Urban VIII, much was made of the fact that Xavier possessed the gift of tongues and that he "spoke to various tribes with ease in their language."[37]

The Biblical context for this gift of tongues is found in the beginning of the book Acts.

Acts 2:5-11: *"Now there were dwelling in Jerusalem Jews, devout men from every nation under heaven. 6 And at this sound the multitude came together, and they were bewildered, because each one was hearing them speak in his own language. 7 And they were amazed and astonished, saying, "Are not all these who are speaking Galileans? 8 And how is it that we hear, each of us in his own native language? 9 Parthians and Medes and Elamites and residents of Mesopotamia, Judea and Cappadocia, Pontus and Asia, 10 Phrygia and Pamphylia, Egypt and the parts of Libya belonging to Cyrene, and visitors from Rome, 11 both Jews and proselytes, Cretans and Arabians—we hear them telling in our own tongues the mighty works of God."*

3) **Heavenly Language In the Church (Interpretation Needed)**

A tongue given in the church is primarily for the unbeliever, but is also for the encouragement of the believers

---

[37] Eddie L. Hyatt, 2000 Years of Charismatic Christianity, 62

present. With this gift, an individual in the church will give a tongue (heavenly language) then someone will come and give an interpretation they have received from the Holy Spirit. In this scenario we see two gifts in action, the tongue and the interpretation.

1 Corinthians 14:6-13: *"Now, brothers, if I come to you speaking in tongues, how will I benefit you unless I bring you some revelation or knowledge or prophecy or teaching? 7 If even lifeless instruments, such as the flute or the harp, do not give distinct notes, how will anyone know what is played? 8 And if the bugle gives an indistinct sound, who will get ready for battle? 9 So with yourselves, if with your tongue you utter speech that is not intelligible, how will anyone know what is said? For you will be speaking into the air. 10 There are doubtless many different languages in the world, and none is without meaning, 11 but if I do not know the meaning of the language, I will be a foreigner to the speaker and the speaker a foreigner to me. 12 So with yourselves, since you are eager for manifestations of the Spirit, strive to excel in building up the church. 13 Therefore, one who speaks in a tongue should pray that he may interpret."*

1 Corinthians 14:22-25: *"Thus tongues are a sign not for believers but for unbelievers, while prophecy is a sign not for unbelievers but for believers. If, therefore, the whole church comes together and all speak in tongues, and outsiders or unbelievers enter, will they not say that you are out of your minds? But if all prophesy, and an unbeliever or outsider enters, he is convicted by all, he is called to account by all, the* *secrets of his heart are disclosed, and so, falling on his face, he will worship God and declare that God is really among you."*

Interpretation of Tongues

When a believer in a church stands up and comes forward with a tongue for the entire body, it benefits no one if there is no interpretation to follow. Paul instructs the one who brings the tongue to the body, is to pray that there is an interpretation given.

1 Corinthian 14:13: *"Therefore, one who speaks in a tongue should pray that he may interpret."*

When there is a tongue given with an interpretation, this is a sign for the unbeliever. They clearly see that God is in the midst of the people.

1 Corinthians 14:22: *"Thus tongues are a sign not for believers but for unbelievers."*

How to Release The Gifts of the Spirit in Your Life

1) Wait on the Lord and ask for a filling of the Holy Spirit.

Praying to be filled with the Holy Spirit should be done daily. Paul speaks to this reality in Ephesians 5:18, *"And do not get drunk with wine, for that is debauchery, but be filled with the Spirit."* Paul's admonition to be filled with the Holy Spirit is a lot more than a one time experience, but it is a daily filling.

2) Understand and believe that the gifts are from the Holy Spirit.
3) Ask for the gifts in your life (1 Corinthians 14:1).

4) Receive the gifts by grace.

Activate them by faith, step out, take a risk, and be humble!

Prayer:
Father, I thank you for sending your Holy Spirit. Holy Spirit, I thank you for empowering your church with gifts. Please increase your activity in my life. I commit to eagerly desire a move of the Spirit in my life, and to flow in the gifts of the Spirit. I bless you, Holy Spirit. Teach me how to walk in your gifts. I ask that you would bring people into my life who can help me grow in this area. Increase your presence in my life.

Activation:
Our heavenly Father desires to give you the Holy Spirit in full, and the Holy Spirit longs to flow through you with His gifts. As you ask and pursue intimacy with the Holy Spirit, step out in faith and ask Him to activate these gifts within you.

> **Luke 11:13:** *"If you then, who are evil, know how to give good gifts to your children, how much more will the heavenly Father give the Holy Spirit to those who ask him!"*
> **Romans 12:6:** *Having gifts that differ according to the grace given to us, let us use them: if prophecy, in proportion to our faith.*

1) Ask the Holy Spirit to release a word of wisdom or knowledge in your workplace. Step out in faith and take a risk. Start with small risks.

2) Ask the Holy Spirit for a prophetic word for a friend. Write it down and give it to them in a card or send it in a text.

3) Ask the Holy Spirit to give you prophetic insight into the lives of your children.
Wait upon the Lord in prayer and write down what you feel He says. Once you get a sense of what He is saying, pray over your children.

Chapter 7
The Gift of Prophecy

The gift of prophecy has shaped my life. Even this book's writing has resulted from the gift of prophetic encouragement. That which we honour, God will give us more. Over the last twenty years, I have received countless prophetic words; words that have guided, encouraged, protected, and called me into what God has for my life. Without these encouraging and comforting words, who knows where I would be today? One of the greatest gifts you can give someone is the gift of encouragement.

Why has God given us the gift of prophecy? We find the purpose and reason the Holy Spirit has given this gift in Paul's letter to the Corinthians.

1 Corinthians 14:3: *"On the other hand, the one who prophesies speaks to people for their upbuilding and encouragement and consolation."*

Paul gives three functions of New Testament prophecy:
1) Building up
2) Encouragement
3) Consolation or Comfort

There is such a spirit of discouragement in this day in age. One of the leading causes for this discouragement is a lack of clear vision in life. We need the gift of prophecy to build one another up. The prophetic can bring great clarity to one's life. In one of Paul's pastoral letters to Timothy, his spiritual son, Paul encourages him to use his prophetic words spoken in the past to wage warfare in his current situation.

1 Timothy 1:18: *"This charge I entrust to you, Timothy, my child, in accordance with the prophecies previously made about you, that by them you may wage the good warfare."*

What an incredible verse! We need the gift of prophecy so that we can wage good warfare. As a child, life is great, filled with playing and fun, with very few things to worry about, but as you grow older, things get a little more complicated. As I came into my twenties, life was great; I was learning who I was and what direction I hoped to take in life. By my mid-twenties, I realized that life would not look as I thought it would. There are real struggles, problems, and difficulties, bills to pay, broken relationships, and shattered dreams are all part of the journey. The Christian walk is a difficult one. I wanted to walk in all God had for me and follow Him in all I do. I wanted to be a person of integrity. Into my mid-thirties, life continued with many disappointments, hurts, and unexpected deaths of loved ones. I love the title of Eugene Peterson's book, "A Long Obedience in the Same Direction;" this is precisely what the Christian life is. Amidst life's ups and downs, the Holy Spirit has given the gift of prophecy so that we can wage warfare with the promises of God. Prophecy calls out the destiny in each of us and encourages us to continue in the things of God. It builds our faith that God is with us and cares for us.

Over the last twenty years, I have kept a box full of prophetic words of encouragement that people have given me. A couple times a year, I will go back to these notes and read over them; doing this brings life to my spirit and I am built up in my inner man. Sometimes, questions arise: why have I not seen these things come to pass? Yet, I am still encouraged to continue in the fight to see the promises of God released over my life.

For my 30th birthday, Becky gave me an incredible gift! She contacted all of my family, friends and mentors, and asked each one of them to write me a prophetic word of encouragement. On the morning of my birthday, I came down the stairs to our kitchen table covered in words and prayers. Five years later, I am still reading over these and being so encouraged by them. These words wage war on the flaming darts of the enemy, and call me into the destiny God has for me. What a gift!

We are all encouraged to pursue the gift of prophecy. Paul implores the church to do this!

1 Corinthians 14:1: *"Pursue love, and earnestly desire the spiritual gifts, especially that you may prophesy."*

While on staff at a church, I was in charge of the prayer teams. These teams were trained to hear the voice of God. When people came forward for prayer, they were to encounter a living God who could speak directly into their situation.

When ministering to others during these times, it was standard practice to wait a few moments in silence to listen to what Jesus wanted to say to them before praying out loud. Prophetic prayer cuts through the details and worries of our lives and goes straight to the heart of the matter. It releases hope, encouragement, comfort and builds up the body of Christ. No one is immune to the difficulties of this world, therefore, we all need to be built up in our faith; a prophetic word will cut through the noise and discouragement.

While getting my haircut recently, I was able to hear some of my hairdresser's life story. We had the normal small talk for a bit and then I asked her if she enjoyed her job. She sighed heavily and said, "That's a long story." She went on to tell me that she grew up in Afghanistan and had always dreamed about becoming a surgeon, because of the nature of the country, her family fled to Pakistan for a few years. After things in Kabul, the capital city of Afghanistan, settled down, they were able to return. This was a major interruption in the plans she had for her life. In 2009, her family moved to Canada, at which point she and her husband began having children. She was never able to pursue her life's dream of being a surgeon. I could see her sadness and disappointment. As I went to pay for my haircut, I shared with her that I was a Christian and while she was sharing her story with me I asked the Holy Spirit if He wanted to say anything to her. (He always wants to say something!) The Holy Spirit said, "Tell her that I see her, that I have not forgotten about her, and that the dreams that she has in her heart are from me. Tell her that I am not distant from her, but that I am near to her." The Salon was empty so I took the opportunity to pray for her. Her entire countenance changed, she was smiling and very encouraged. Even through many disappointments and discouragements, God has a plan for her life. I hope and pray she is one day able to pursue the passions that Jesus has planted in her heart.

Giving a Prophetic Word

When praying for others and releasing a prophetic word over them, the Bible lays out guidelines and protocols for us to follow.

Guideline # 1: Make Love Your Aim

Paul teaches us in 1 Corinthians 13 that we need to function in love.

1 Corinthians 13:4-7: *"Love is patient and kind; love does not envy or boast; it is not arrogant or rude. It does not insist on its own way; it is not irritable or resentful; it does not rejoice at wrongdoing, but rejoices with the truth. Love bears all things, believes all things, hopes all things, endures all things."*

Can we be people who walk in love in everything we do? Can we be a people who are secure enough in who we are that we don't need to puff ourselves up by using the gifts that the Spirit has given us for selfish gain?

Guideline # 2: Always be Encouraging (1 Corinthians 14:3)

We share a prophetic word with others to love them well. We do this by building them up, encouraging them and comforting them. If you ever encounter someone who does not do this in sharing a prophetic word, you can immediately take it and *flush it down the toilet.* My default is to give a lot of grace to people, because everyone is learning. If we can all exert a little maturity and give people the benefit-of-the-doubt, there may even be a lot less hurt in the church today.

Sometimes, people share words with others and are completely off base, stirring up fear and manipulation. Other times, some people must learn to walk in love as they deliver a word. The words that they share can be accurate, but their delivery needs some work. Again, let's give grace to those around us.

Kris Vallotton shares a great rule of thumb for giving a prophetic word, "We are to mine gold buried in the dirt of people's lives and find hidden treasure. If we see negative things in the life of the person we are ministering to, we need to ask the Holy Spirit for the answer to the problem we discern. This will result in people receiving God's grace and allowing him to deal with the issue."[38]

If we discern something in someone's life that is not of God, ask the Holy Spirit if it is for you to bring a corrective word, and if so, ask if this is the right time. A corrective word can sometimes be hard to give and to receive. Bringing correction or a difficult word can be done with love, kindness and gentleness. If you believe God is asking you to give a corrective or difficult word, ensure that it is bathed in 1 Corinthians 13 love and that the fruit of the Spirit (Galatians 5:22-23) is being deployed. If it is not, don't bother sharing it.

---

[38] Kris Vallotton, School of the Prophets (Bloomington, Minnesota: Chosen Books, 2015) 114

Guideline # 3: Walk in Humility

When it comes to giving a prophetic word, we are all learning and growing in hearing God's voice. No one gets it right every time, and sometimes impure motives creep into our thoughts. When giving prophetic words of encouragement to one another, we must walk in maturity and humility. Encourage the one receiving the word to test it. Write it down, pray, and share it with a mentor if necessary. Walking in a spirit of humility puts your heart in a place that says, "Lord, I want all that you have for me." When giving a prophetic word, say, "I humbly submit this word to you; please test it, pray into it and ask the Holy Spirit if this is for you." Secondly, ask for feedback. Ask questions like, "Does this make sense? Is that encouraging? Are you strengthened in your faith?"

Guideline # 4: Prophesy in Community

Prophesying in community gives room for accountability for the one giving the word, and for the one receiving the word. For the one giving the word, it ensures that they walk in love, encouragement, and humility. We don't need more rogue prophets giving bad prophetic words and damaging the body of Christ. There must be accountability. Sometimes, when receiving a word, there might be an action step that you need to take afterwards. This is again why someone needs to hold you to this word and encourage you to walk in the things that God is calling you to.

Testing a Prophetic Word

Prophecy is one of the greatest gifts of the Spirit of God for His church, however, this gift can cause confusion, hurt and pain. That being said, to avoid any pitfalls, we must **judge** and **weigh** each word. We must be careful in this regard. One of the biggest reasons why there is so much hurt and confusion around the topic of prophecy is because people fail to judge what is being spoken.

1 Thessalonians 5:20-21: *"Do not despise prophecies, but test everything; hold fast to what is good."*

We must take each word we receive and put it under the microscope. We are responsible for testing every word spoken to us, throwing out what is not for us and holding onto what is good. There is a great saying in the prophetic community that "the one receiving the word is more powerful than the one giving the word." The one giving the word is subject to the one receiving the word, because every word must be tested. We have the ability to accept or reject the prophetic word.

We receive a word by saying yes to it in prayer or no to it in prayer. We also receive words by partnering with them in action, not trying to make a prophetic word come to pass, but by taking steps of obedience in that direction. Nothing can stick to your life you don't receive or partner with.

1 Corinthians 14:29: *"Let two or three prophets speak, and let the others weigh what is said."*

Test # 1 - The Written Word of God

The written Word of God is always our standard. It is the rule by which we measure whether a word is from God. What does this mean? It doesn't mean that you will find the exact words in the Bible, but that it will not contradict God's revealed character and nature, or oppose the values and principles in His written word.

Paul states that we must not quench the Spirit and despise prophecy, but we must test everything. That means *everything*; dreams, visions, prophetic words, impressions, angelic visitations, the still small voice, etc. We grieve the heart of God when we outright reject prophecy instead of taking it for what it is and judging it. This is because the gift of prophecy is a gift of the Spirit, and when we despise His gifts, we say, "I don't need the Spirit of God working in my life; I am good without it." This quenches His work in our lives. The writer of Hebrews gives us a great tool to judge and weigh words.

Hebrews 4:12: *"For the word of God is living and active, sharper than any two-edged sword, piercing to the division of soul and of spirit, of joints and of marrow, and discerning the thoughts and intentions of the heart."*

What a beautiful hope we can have in the written word of God; it judges, tests and discerns intentions! Do you want to test prophetic words that have been given to you or others? Submit it to the word of God. Do you want the inward workings of your heart to be tested? Read and meditate on the word of God, and allow it to be the plum line of your heart. Paul gives a clear warning that any other gospel that is preached should be discarded and thrown away.

Galatians in 1:8-9: *"But even if we or an angel from heaven should preach to you a gospel contrary to the one we preached to you, let him be accursed. As we have said before, so now I say again: If anyone is preaching to you a gospel contrary to the one you received, let him be accursed."*

Every word spoken must come under the revealed word of God in the scripture.

I love what Graham Cooke says, "It is vital to note that we are building our lives on scripture and not on prophecy. In the event of a clash, we abandon the prophetic word in favour of scripture, the revealed word of God. We must be especially careful that the substance of the extra-biblical revelation does not contradict the Bible, but is in accord with the revealed message."[39]

Test # 2 - Upbuild, Encourage and Comfort

The New Testament function and purpose of prophecy is to upbuild, encourage and comfort. As previously said, Paul speaks to this reality in 1 Corinthians 14:3. New Testament prophecy should never discourage, tear down, put fear in others (contrary to the fear of the Lord), or bring confusion, chaos, or condemnation. Even though sometimes the prophetic word might be hard to hear, and a correction might be brought, it must always end in encouragement and building up.

---

[39] Graham Cooke, Developing Your Prophetic Gifting (Tonbridge, Kent: Sovereign World International, 1994) 151

Test # 3 - Test the Spirit of the Word

1 John 4:1-3: *"Beloved, do not believe every spirit, but test the spirits to see whether they are from God, for many false prophets have gone out into the world. By this you know the Spirit of God: every spirit that confesses that Jesus Christ has come in the flesh is from God, and every spirit that does not confess Jesus is not from God. This is the spirit of the antichrist, which you heard was coming and now is in the world already."*

We must be careful in discerning the spirit of the word. John gives us instructions to test the spirits; the content can be correct, but the spirit is wrong. In the book of Acts, we see this playing out before our eyes.

Acts 16:16-18: *"As we were going to the place of prayer, we were met by a slave girl who had a spirit of divination and brought her owners much gain by fortune-telling. She followed Paul and us, crying out, "These men are servants of the Most High God, who proclaim to you the way of salvation." And this she kept doing for many days. Paul, having become greatly annoyed, turned and said to the spirit, "I command you in the name of Jesus Christ to come out of her." And it came out that very hour."*

We need to weigh the spirit behind the word because we may end up being deceived. Discernment may be the essential gift we need in the body of Christ today. Many voices and agendas are not from God. Interestingly, some are not hidden anymore; they are in plain sight. We must discern which spirit they are from, or many will be deceived.

There is an internal knowing and sensing when testing the spirit behind the word. When something is of demonic origin, there will be fear, lack of peace, and sometimes even a desire to vomit. One of the indicators that the word is not of God is that there is an uneasy feeling or sense. There is peace, hope, and joy when the Holy Spirit is the origin.

Prophetic voice, Stacey Campell says, "Testing the spirits is a complex procedure, there is no one single test."[40] She offers three tests:

1) Biblical Orthodoxy (What one believes)
    - We must be students of the word. This is no fluffy saying, we have to know the word of God. Most believers would be hard pressed to say they need not be ashamed when it comes to handling the word of truth. 2
    - **2 Timothy 2:15:** *Do your best to present yourself to God as one approved, a worker who has no need to be ashamed, rightly handling the word of truth.*
    - When we affirm that Jesus is the Christ, the Messiah, we are affirming an entire belief system, we are affirming every last thing about who he claimed to be and what the word of God says about him. What do we claim to be true about who Christ is?

---

[40] Stacey Campbell, Ecstatic Prophecy (Grand Rapids, Michigan: Chosen, 2008) 127-139

2) Biblical Behaviour (How one behaves)
   - Is the fruit of Spirit evident? (Galatians 5:22-23) Is the character of Jesus present?
     Matthew 7:18-20: *A healthy tree cannot bear bad fruit, nor can a diseased tree bear good fruit. Every tree that does not bear good fruit is cut down and thrown into the fire. Thus you will recognize them by their fruits.*
3) Biblical Content (The accuracy of the prophecy)
   - The prophecy is true
   - The prophecy is speaking to one's future potential
   - The prophecy is right and wrong (mixture)
     - There is part of the word that is correct and part of the word that is wrong.
   - The prophecy is false

Test # 4 - Does it Confirm what you Know to be True?

Another way to test a prophetic word is by comparing them to past prophetic words or what you already know to be true.

Test # 5 - Judge the Word in Community

When judging a prophetic word, we want to make sure that we bring others into the process. This cannot be overstated; we must discern with our leaders, mentors or close friends. This is especially true with directional words. When judging the word we must judge the interpretation of the word and the application of the word.

Four Possible Options

When given a prophetic word, we have four options of how to receive or handle it.

Option #1 - Receiving a Word

First, we can receive a word with gladness. We receive a word by giving God a "yes" in our hearts and then beginning to partner with that word. Take steps in faith toward it. Maybe someone is encouraging you to follow the desires that God has put in your heart. That may mean buying tools and landing a job with a home builder to begin learning to build homes, or going to school to become a doctor. Or maybe you have a heart for people experiencing homelessness in your community, so you partner with a shelter in your city. Prophetic words can also be geared towards the season of life the Lord has you in. Someone might encourage you to press into receiving the Father's heart because you need a fresh revelation of your sonship in Christ. In turn, you begin to spend time in the secret place, receiving the love of the Father.

Option #2 - Shelving a Word

Secondly, we can save a prophetic word. There might be nothing wrong with the word; it lines up with the character of God, is encouraging, and witnesses with your spirit, but you are unsure of the timing. Or it's a great word, but you need to know if it is for you. This is when we say in our hearts, "Lord, have your will and your way. I don't know what to do with this word, but I'm not saying "no." I will put it on the shelf for now and see what comes." What might begin to happen is you receive more words that line up with that word on the shelf, and so in a year or two years, or maybe longer, you begin to partner with that word. Sometimes, we receive a word that seems entirely out of the blue, but it ignites something in us, and over time, it starts to grow; we take it off the shelf and begin to see God move in incredible ways.

Option #3 - Flushing a Prophetic Word

In my life, flushing a prophetic word happens the least of all. I want to walk in such humility with the Lord that He is willing to speak in all areas of my life. I will write down every prophetic word I get unless it is completely off. Sometimes, when we are given a prophetic word, we know immediately that the person giving the word isn't trying to be mean or rude, but they just haven't heard right. We can politely say thank you for the word, and then pray, "Lord, whatever is of you, I receive it, and whatever is not of you, I flush it." There are other times, which have been rare in my life, that the word is mean-spirited, rude and discourages me rather than encourages. These are flushed right away. We don't have to give our "yes" to these words. I want to admonish you with the words of Paul: don't despise prophecy if someone gets it wrong or is not operating in the right spirit; test it. You are a powerful person. You are not subject to the one giving you the word, and you are not bound by their words.

Option #4 - Disregarding the Prophetic Word

The final option in response to a prophetic word is to do nothing. Many may miss the call or destiny in their lives when they do not partner or steward the prophetic word, but this is ultimately your choice.

Prayer:

Jesus, would you release the gift of prophecy in my life today? Use me to bless others and build up your church. Holy Spirit, I submit to your leadership in my life and ask that you would prompt me throughout the day to release your prophetic words wherever I am.

Activation:

Pick a friend or family member. Ask the Holy Spirit for a prophetic word, or picture for them. Let them know that they are loved by God today. Share the word with them and ask for feedback. Remember the more often we can get feedback, the more we can grow in accuracy.

Chapter 8
Am I Hearing God?

Hebrews 5:14: (NKJV) *"But solid food belongs to those who are of full age, that is, those who by reason of use have their senses exercised to discern both good and evil."*

1 Corinthians 13:9-12: *"For we know in part and we prophesy in part, but when the perfect comes, the partial will pass away. When I was a child, I spoke like a child, I thought like a child, I reasoned like a child. When I became a man, I gave up childish ways. 12 For now we see in a mirror dimly, but then face to face. Now I know in part; then I shall know fully, even as I have been fully known."*

We never fully arrive at hearing God perfectly all the time, however, we can get to a place where we recognize the voice of the Lord more clearly. Some are fearful about what or who they will hear talking to them. God is more committed to speaking to you than you are to hearing Him. God wants to talk to you; our job is to discern who we hear. Learning to hear God's voice is a journey I have intentionally been on for over fifteen years. There are times when I hear God as clear as day, and there are times when I struggle to understand what He is saying. Don't beat yourself up. Be patient, and remember that you are learning and growing. Keep on taking time to listen to

His voice and be silent in His presence. When we know what His voice sounds like in the quiet, we will begin to recognize it when there are noises or distractions around us.

When learning to hear God's voice, one of the most common questions is, "Am I hearing God, or are these just my thoughts?" Primarily, there are four sources of the thoughts that go through our mind.

Paul understands that there are other "voices" and "thoughts" that we hear throughout our day. He commands us to destroy any thought that is not of God.

2 Corinthians 10:5-6: *"We destroy arguments and every lofty opinion raised against the knowledge of God, and take every thought captive to obey Christ, being ready to punish every disobedience, when your obedience is complete."*

The Four Primary Sources of the Voices we Hear
1) **The World**

Brad Jersak states these voices are "the barrage of ungodly messages that we hear through the media, educational and political systems, advertising campaigns and so on."[41] Paul states that we must have our minds renewed so that we can discern what is of Him and what is not of Him.

Romans 12:2: *"Do not be conformed to this world, but be transformed by the renewal of your mind, that by testing you may discern what the will of God is, what is good and acceptable and perfect."*

---

[41] Brad Jersak, Can You Hear Me, 74

The ways of this world and the ways of God are opposite of each other. The Lord's voice is often harder to hear when I am on social media too much. I find I need to take a break from social media and realign my heart to His voice again when it seems as though I cannot hear Him clearly. The word of God cuts through the voices of this world as Jesus points out.

John 17:17: *"Sanctify them in the truth; your word is truth."*

2) **The Holy Spirit**

The Holy Spirit lives in us, and His voice is the one we want to be hearing regularly. We want to have His voice wash over us and speak to our hearts. The Spirit of God lives in us.

1 Corinthians 6:19: *"Or do you not know that your body is a temple of the Holy Spirit within you, whom you have from God? You are not your own."*

The apostle Paul also says that the Holy Spirit bears witness with our spirits that we are God's children. Another way you could say this is that He speaks *to* our spirits.

Galatians 4:6-7: *"And because you are sons, God has sent the Spirit of his Son into our hearts, crying, "Abba! Father!" So you are no longer a slave, but a son, and if a son, then an heir through God."*

One of the first times I remember hearing God's voice was when I was nineteen years old, driving in my car and listening to a sermon by David Wilkerson called, "Getting to know the Holy Spirit." At one point in the sermon, David Wilkerson began to talk about being sons and daughters of God; I began to weep uncontrollably as the Holy Spirit began to witness to my spirit that I am a son of my Father in heaven.

The Holy Spirit brings to remembrance the things that Jesus said. He also brings to memory the scriptures. The Holy Spirit will never condemn you, but He will convict you. The Spirit will be kind as He deals with you.

Romans 2:4: *"Or do you presume on the riches of his kindness and forbearance and patience, not knowing that God's kindness is meant to lead you to repentance?"*

3) Evil Spirits

The voices of evil spirits or demonic voices often sound like ours and are the easiest to hear. They usually consist of negative thoughts and temptation. We must take all these thoughts captive and make them bow down to Jesus.

Joy Dawson says, "The voices of the demonic spirits are often loud, urgent and insistent, as Satan is always trying to precipitate a crisis and trying to get us to act hastily. Whereas the voice of the Lord is often quiet but persistent, motivating us to quietly wait and listen."[42]

It is easy to recognize these voices, but sometimes challenging to let them go. They will often create fear and doubt. When stepping out in faith, they often tell you, "You are making a bad decision." These voices will be the loudest when

---

[42] Joy Dawson, Forever Ruined For the Ordinary, 37

trying to follow the Lord during significant transitions, giant faith steps, and believing the Lord to move powerfully. These voices are the loudest in the middle of the night; they come and taunt you. They will rob you of your peace and create fear and uncertainty.

James 4:7: *"Submit yourselves therefore to God. Resist the devil, and he will flee from you."*

Remember that Jesus has *"given you authority to tread on serpents and scorpions, and over all the power of the enemy, and nothing shall hurt you"* (Luke 10:19). Command all demonic voices to be silent in the name of Jesus!

It is easy to decipher between the Holy Spirit and an evil spirit. The hard part is choosing to block out the voice of the enemy.

Here are some clues to determine whether you are hearing the enemy or the Holy Spirit:

The Enemy Condemns
You're a failure.
You will never succeed.
You're stupid.
Does God really love me?
All you do is sin.
God is causing all your pain.

The Spirit Convicts us of Who Christ has Made us to Be

You are forgiven.

You are righteous.

You are created in Christ Jesus for good works.

You are my son/daughter.

The Spirit will call us to make wrong things right in our lives.

The Spirit calls us into our Christ-given identity.

The Spirit will call us to a higher standard.

The Holy Spirit often sounds like our voice, but the content of what is said is what separates it and points to the source of the Holy Spirit.

4) Our Unrenewed Thoughts

The renewed mind is one of the most important things to go after in the Christian walk. Thankfully, the Holy Spirit works inside us, sanctifying us and making us more like Christ. Often, we will hear the voice of our unrenewed mind; our flesh, but we need to follow after the Spirit.

Philippians 4:8: *"Finally, brothers, whatever is true, whatever is honorable, whatever is just, whatever is pure, whatever is lovely, whatever is commendable, if there is any excellence, if there is anything worthy of praise, think about these things."*

It is essential to guard our minds; we must depend on the Spirit of God to help us in our weakness.

Tools to Discern God's Voice

1) It will Never Contradict the Scripture

The Holy Scripture is God's word. It is our standard in relating to God, understanding God, and knowing His character and nature. When discerning God's voice, if we hear something contrary to God's character and nature revealed in scripture, we are not hearing God.

After the death of Moses, God commissions Joshua to become the next leader of Israel. In His commissioning statement, God declares this over Joshua:

Joshua 1:8: *"This Book of the Law shall not depart from your mouth, but you shall meditate on it day and night, so that you may be careful to do according to all that is written in it. For then you will make your way prosperous, and then you will have good success."*

2) Peace Over Fear

When we hear God's voice and follow His leading, it will often require faith which can be scary or nerve-wracking; this is not the fear I am talking about. When we follow His voice and know it is Him, there will be peace that accompanies this voice.

Isaiah 26:3: *You keep him in perfect peace whose mind is stayed on you because he trusts in you.*
Philippians 4:4-7: *"Rejoice in the Lord always; again I will say, rejoice. Let your reasonableness be known to everyone. The Lord is at hand; do not be anxious about anything, but in*

everything by prayer and supplication with thanksgiving let your requests be made known to God. And the peace of God, which surpasses all understanding, will guard your hearts and your minds in Christ Jesus.

3) Does it Bring Glory to God and Draw out Faith?

Does what you are hearing point you to Jesus? Does it make you lean into Him more, or does it make you prideful? Does it have the potential to further God's kingdom? Is it self-centered? Does it make much of you?

Just because you have heard God speak and call you to something doesn't mean it will be easy, but most often, it is the exact opposite. It will usually require great faith to step into what He is asking you to do. This is another sign that God is speaking to you. He wants to bring us to the end of ourselves so that He can move. That's why Paul states:

2 Corinthians 12:9-10: *"But he said to me, "My grace is sufficient for you, for my power is made perfect in weakness." Therefore, I will boast all the more gladly of my weaknesses, so that the power of Christ may rest upon me. For the sake of Christ, then, I am content with weaknesses, insults, hardships, persecutions, and calamities. For when I am weak, then I am strong."*

There will be times when what the Lord is asking us requires an immense degree of faith, and we have to walk moment by moment, listening to His voice. These are challenging times, but incredibly rewarding as you walk in intimacy with the Lord and get to see Him move. Even in these times, the dominant sense in your heart will be peace.

4) Does it Bear Good Fruit?

Sometimes, seeing the fruit of listening to God's voice takes time. We don't always see the outworkings of God right away or the fruit of our obedience, but with time it will be evident.

John 15:16: *"You did not choose me, but I chose you and appointed you that you should go and bear fruit and that your fruit should abide, so that whatever you ask the Father in my name, he may give it to you."*

5) Share with a Friend, Mentor or Leader

If you are wondering or doubting whether you have heard God, be sure to share it with a friend, leader, family member or pastor. I have a few friends I share with, including my wife, the things that I feel or sense from the Lord. It is always good to hear what those close to you think when you are unsure. Make sure that the individuals are mature in their faith and understand the Lord speaking.

Prayer:

God, I thank you that you are more committed to speaking to your children than we are committed to listening. In the name of Jesus, I silence all other voices and say "Speak Holy Spirit, I want to hear you!"

Activation:

1) Continue to cultivate your God awareness. Spend today praying short prayers as you go about your day: "Holy Spirit, I honour you. Holy Spirit, I yield to you. Holy Spirit, fill me."

2) Renew your mind by meditating on scripture. These verses are a great place to start: Philippians 2:1-11, Psalm 119, John 17:17, Psalm 1, Colossians 1:15-19, Revelation 4, Ephesians 1 and 2.

3) Pick a friend you haven't talked to in a while, spend time listening to the Lord and ask Him what He wants to speak to them. Send them an encouraging email or text message.

Chapter 9
The Good Shepherd

John 10:1-5: (NIV) *"Very truly I tell you Pharisees, anyone who does not enter the sheep pen by the gate, but climbs in by some other way, is a thief and a robber. The one who enters by the gate is the shepherd of the sheep. The gatekeeper opens the gate for him, and the sheep listen to his voice. He calls his own sheep by name and leads them out. When he has brought out all his own, he goes on ahead of them, and his sheep follow him because they know his voice. But they will never follow a stranger; in fact, they will run away from him because they do not recognize a stranger's voice."*

John 10:27: *"My sheep hear my voice, and I know them, and they follow me."*

His Leadership

As we go on the journey of hearing God's voice, one of the foundational passages of scripture is found in John 10. Jesus speaks of His leadership compared to the leaders of the day, primarily the Pharisees. Understanding and knowing the leadership of Jesus is of utmost importance in following His voice. Following Jesus is the most rewarding commitment you will ever make, but it will cost you everything. To know that we can trust Jesus and that He is good in every situation is an absolute necessity.

The Bible was written thousands of years ago and into a completely different culture than we live in today. Thus, we must understand these words not in our 21st-century minds and cultures, but in the context of the culture it was written in. Understanding John 10 in the context of a Palestinian Shepherd is essential. Biblical Scholar and New Testament Professor at Asbury Theological Seminary, Craig Keener shares, "A shepherd in the first century would spend much of his life with his flock. He would know his sheep intimately. Leading them by streams, allowing them to stop and drink water, and going on journeys to find fresh grass; there were hills they would have to climb together, some sheep would have a difficult time, and the shepherd would carry them. It was even said that the shepherd would know each of his sheep by name. The sheepfold was a pen where the shepherds would bring their sheep at night, protecting them from predators or getting lost or stolen by thieves. Many different flocks of sheep would be mixed, and in the morning, each shepherd would call their sheep, and the sheep would follow."[43]

I grew up on a dairy farm in Southern Manitoba, Canada. My Grandpa and Grandma and my Dad and Mom owned the farm together. I spent a lot of time helping my Dad as a little boy, and my responsibilities increased as I grew older. My chores consisted of laying down straw for the cows to rest on, feeding the cows and calves, shoveling a lot of manure, and

---

[43] Craig Keener, IVP Bible Background Commentary: New Testament. (Downers Grove, Illinois: InterVarsity Press, 1993) 290

various other tasks around the farm. As you spend time around the animals, you learn the intricacies of each cow and calf. You need to be careful around certain cows because they might kick you. You learned how each cow looked and the different marks on each one of them. Even though I was a young boy, there was a sense that I knew the animals.

The shepherd and sheep relationship was intricately woven together; they knew each other intimately. Watching a shepherd lead their sheep is a beautiful thing. The sheep can be scattered throughout the pasture, far away from sight. When the shepherd begins to call, the sheep's head pops up from feeding on the grass, and they run to their master. They know their master's voice and trust it completely. They may not be able to see him, but they can hear him.

For Jesus to use the metaphor of a shepherd and sheep for His leadership towards His people is not unusual. God often used this metaphor in the scripture. The Prophets of the Old Testament referred to the leaders of God's people as shepherds. Ezekiel 34, Zechariah 9-14, and Jeremiah 23 are just a few examples.

A famous scripture that believers often memorize, is a picture of the leadership of Jesus.

Psalm 23: *"The Lord is my shepherd; I shall not want. He makes me lie down in green pastures. He leads me beside still waters. He restores my soul. He leads me in paths of righteousness for his name's sake. Even though I walk through the valley of the shadow of death, I will fear no evil, for you are with me; your rod and your staff, they comfort me. You prepare a table before me in the presence of my enemies; you anoint my* *head with oil; my cup overflows. Surely goodness and mercy shall follow me all the days of my life, and I shall dwell in the house of the Lord forever."*

What a beautiful picture of the guidance of Jesus. He takes care of the sheep, leading them perfectly to streams and through valleys, protecting and comforting them. The direction of Jesus is perfect; hearing His voice and obeying Him is where we want to posture ourselves.

As we come back to John 10:4 Jesus says, *"When he has brought out all his sheep, he goes before them."* The Palestinian shepherd would lead his sheep by going out before them, or go ahead of them; he would not drive them and push or prod them from behind. The sheep would follow because they knew his voice. Isn't it beautiful that we can trust the leading of Jesus because He goes before us? Wherever He is calling us, He is already there. He is there if He calls us to the mountaintops; if He calls us into the valley, He is already there. When we are following His voice and leading, there is no place we can go without Him. This should bring the utmost comfort to our hearts and peace to our souls. I love what Dan Bauman says, "The safest place to be is in the centre of God's will."[44]

Jesus is a safe leader. He is the One who knows His sheep intimately, the One who goes before them and sacrifices for the sheep. They can trust His voice; they can trust His calling. Sheep are prone to wandering; there are many dangers, cliffs and rocks, open lands, they could get lost, robbers could steal them, and wolves and wild animals may attack to kill

---

[44] Dan Bauman, "Missions"

them. The sheep's safety is directly connected to the voice of their shepherd. Our shepherd's voice is knowable and heard. We are kept safe by His voice. Sheep following their shepherd is directly connected to the voice of the shepherd. We must know and recognize His voice in order to be led.

Craig Keener states, "Jesus describes himself as the Good Shepherd. This phrase sums up so much: the close, personal relationship between himself and each of his followers; the absolute security they have in him, his leadership and guidance; his constant company; his unfailing care."[45]

Theologian Leon Morris suggests, "While it is right to think of the shepherd in these terms, we must not neglect that he is also the one who is in control; he is the ruler of his people, he is our Lord, what he says we must obey."[46]

As followers of Jesus this begs the question: are we going to allow Jesus to be the Lord of our lives? Are we going to listen and submit to His voice?

His Voice

How could we follow our leader (our shepherd), if we don't know His voice? How can we be the hands and feet of Jesus without hearing His voice? How can we walk in our true identity if we don't know what our shepherd is speaking to us? Our leader has a voice, and we can know and hear it.

---

[45] Keener, IVP Bible Background Commentary: New Testament, 290

[46] Leon Morris, NICNT, The Gospel According to John. (Grand Rapids, Michigan: WM. B. Eerdmans Publishing Company) 502-503

John 10:3-5: *"To him, the gatekeeper opens. The sheep hear his voice, and he calls his own sheep by name and leads them out. 4 When he has brought out all his own, he goes before them, and the sheep follow him, for they know his voice. 5 A stranger they will not follow, but they will flee from him, for they do not know the voice of strangers."*

It is in this context that we can seek direction from our Lord, and we can trust His voice. Let the words of Jesus be a comfort to you as you lean into His voice. He is there to be heard.

Seeking the Lord for Direction

Psalm 32:8-9: *"I will instruct you and teach you in the way you should go; I will counsel you with my eye upon you. Be not like a horse or a mule, without understanding, which must be curbed with bit and bridle, or it will not stay near you."*

Jeremiah 10:23: *"I know, O Lord, that the way of man is not in himself, that it is not in man who walks to direct his steps."*

You could define the Christian life by the word "faith." We know from the writer of Hebrews that it is impossible to please God if we are not walking in faith (Hebrews 11:6). Whenever we seek the Lord for direction in our lives, it is an opportunity to step out in faith and trust that the Lord will guide us. Each person listed in the "hall of faith" walked by faith; they believed the Lord spoke to them, and they went on a wild adventure. Abraham is a great example; the father of the faith. He gathered his family and his belongings and started in the direction that God would show him (Genesis 12:1-3).

Walking by faith is not easy, because we are walking with our spiritual eyes rather than walking with our natural eyes. We need help seeing where we are going, and we must trust the Lord in every step. There have been times when I have stepped out in faith, and it seemed like an utter failure. There have been other times when I have taken a faith step and seen amazing things happen; yet in both circumstances, God remained faithful. Sometimes, we don't immediately see the fruit of our faith step; stick with it, and the time will come to see the fulfillment come to pass.

We find great encouragement and comfort in the words of the prophet Habakkuk.

Habakkuk 2:3-4: *"For still the vision awaits its appointed time; it hastens to the end—it will not lie. If it seems slow, wait for it; it will surely come; it will not delay. "Behold, his soul is puffed up; it is not upright within him, but the righteous shall live by his faith."*

I think the church is (mostly) bored because our Christian walk has been dumbed down to taking in a service on a Sunday morning and winning the culture war. Risk-taking has been completely removed from the Christian journey. We have become a church playing defense, trying not to be "contaminated" by the world, rather than living on the offensive, expanding the Kingdom of God by living out our wildest faith! Are you taking steps of faith that would require God to move in miraculous ways? Most of our lives are too comfortable to need God to move in any sort of way; we never take risks that require Him to come through. I believe that if the church is going to walk in its true identity, we will need to take a page out of Abraham's book, we will need to take radical risks and start burning our "backup" plans. Backup plans keep the church in bondage to a faithless Christianity. It's time to put all our eggs in one basket and walk by faith like the heroes of old. God is not looking for success; He is looking for radical obedience. Hearing the voice of God and walking in radical obedience will shock you out of your boredom; it will forever ruin you for the ordinary!

Another story that comes to mind is the story of Elisha's calling in the book of Kings.

1 Kings 19:19-21: *"So he departed from there and found Elisha the son of Shaphat, who was plowing with twelve yoke of oxen in front of him, and he was with the twelfth. Elijah passed by him and cast his cloak upon him. And he left the oxen and ran after Elijah and said, "Let me kiss my father and my mother, and then I will follow you." And he said to him, "Go back again, for what have I done to you?" And he returned from following him and took the yoke of oxen and sacrificed them and boiled their flesh with the yokes of the oxen and gave it to the people, and they ate. Then he arose and went after Elijah and assisted him."*

What is happening here? God calls Elisha into the prophetic ministry by Elijah throwing his cloak on Elisha. Without hesitation, Elisha takes his entire livelihood as a farmer and burns his plow to cook meat on it. This must have been a glorious barbeque! Elisha burns everything; there is no trace of his former life left. This is how we should be following after Jesus. No plan B's. God, what are you saying? I will do it; I will follow. This is the faith that changes history; this is the faith that defies the status quo of boring Christianity; this is the faith that pleases God. My friend Don Gilman once said, "Is the life you are living worth Jesus dying for?"[47] The life worth living is the life walking by faith. He then said, "Faith is spelled "RISK." Everyone wants to change the world, but no one wants to take the risk that it will require to change it. Don laid out this challenge, "If your life is worth dying for, then it must be worth you living for."[48] There is story after story of radical faith and obedience in the Bible; Jesus is calling every one who follows Him to this type of life, and it's certainly NOT boring!

In journeying with the God of the universe, we know that everything He has planned for us is always good, but it is certainly not safe or boring; it will cost us absolutely everything.

God is Trustworthy

There are a few reasons why believers have failed in radical obedience. One of them is that they don't believe that God is trustworthy. Can they trust God with their kids? Can they trust God with their dreams? Do they think that God will provide for all their needs? What is God's will for my life? I

---

[47] Don Gilman, "Evangelism," (Lecture Notes, University of the Nations, November, 2008)

[48] Gilman, "Evangelism"

love what Dan Bauman says, "God is more committed to fulfilling his will in my life than I am committed to finding it."[49] This has multiple implications. We don't have to worry or stress about it; we can trust that His will for our life will come to pass as we walk in radical obedience. It also means He desires to share His will and plans with us if we listen. We probably won't get to see the whole picture at once, most likely just as much as we need.

This truth is also connected to hearing God's voice. He is more committed to speaking to us than we are committed to hearing His voice. He desires to share the secrets of His heart with us. The psalmist writes in Psalm 25:14, *"The friendship of the Lord is for those who fear him, and he makes known to them his covenant."* When we seek the Lord for direction in our lives, we can trust He is faithful to lead and guide us; it might be through wise counsel, a dream, a word, or a scripture. He is the good shepherd!

Here are four ways in which we can seek the Lord for direction in our lives:

1) Stay Connected to Jesus

We must be connected to the one who gives life.

John 15:1-8: *"I am the true vine, and my Father is the gardener. He cuts off every branch in me that bears no fruit, while every branch that does bear fruit he prunes so that it will be even more fruitful. You are already clean because of the*

---

[49] Bauman, "Missions"

word I have spoken to you. Remain in me, as I also remain in you. No branch can bear fruit by itself; it must remain in the vine. Neither can you bear fruit unless you remain in me. "I am the vine; you are the branches. If you remain in me and I in you, you will bear much fruit; apart from me you can do nothing. If you do not remain in me, you are like a branch that is thrown away and withers; such branches are picked up, thrown into the fire and burned. If you remain in me and my words remain in you, ask whatever you wish, and it will be done for you. This is to my Father's glory, that you bear much fruit, showing yourselves to be my disciples."

Jesus tells us the necessity of staying connected to the vine. If we want to bear fruit and prove that we are His disciples, we must remain connected to Him. We cannot treat God like a vending machine where we only meet with Him to give us direction; we are then partnering with a spirit of witchcraft, using God like a fortune teller. Remember, God desires to walk in relationship and intimacy with us. This means we allow Him into all areas of our lives. In all the ways we seek the Lord for direction, staying connected to Him is the most important part. I cannot say this enough, take <u>every</u> decision to the Lord! Parents, raising your kids is a huge task, and we must stay connected to the voice of the Lord for His wisdom in this area. Hearing His voice is imperative in discipline, health decisions, and our children's needs. Each of our children is different and needs different things. Why would we not listen to the voice of God when raising our kids? He knows them better than we do. Young adults going off to college or finding a career, lay your plans before the Lord, and He will guide you. Business owners, take your hiring and other business decisions to the Lord, ask Him about the projects you should take on as a business.

Proverbs 3:5-6: *"Trust in the Lord with all your heart and do not lean on your own understanding. In all your ways acknowledge him, and he will make straight your paths."*

As I look back over my late teens, twenties and early thirties, there have been many difficulties, but it has been incredible to see how the Lord has led me as a single man, as a husband, and as a father. You will never regret involving Jesus in every aspect of your life.

2) Stay Connected to the Church

In the Western world, we pride ourselves in our individuality and independence, and loathe asking for help. "I can do it on my own." We have a tough time involving others in our lives, yet we live in a society that desperately longs for connection and community. We were made to be in community. The fact that God is a triune God speaks to our need for relationships. When it comes to decision-making, wise counsel cannot be overstated. The book of Proverbs is filled with wisdom.

Proverbs 12:15: *"The way of a fool is right in his own eyes, but a wise man listens to advice."*

As we listen to the Lord for direction in our lives, it is wise to have mentors and friends who know you speak into what you sense the Lord is saying. We should also ask others to pray for us and press into listening to the Lord on our behalf. Over the last fifteen years, I have often asked my friends and mentors to listen to the Lord for what He says about my life or my family's life. My community of friends and mentors often confirm that we are hearing the Lord, or that perhaps our timing is off in this season. One of my closest friends and mentors has often encouraged me, "Randall, you have not missed it; you are in the dead centre of the will of God."

In Acts chapter 15, we see what is known as the Jerusalem Council. Many Gentiles were coming to know Jesus, and the Jewish believers were trying to navigate what to do. Should they make them get circumcised according to the Jewish customs and law, or should they let them eat particular meat that was not a Jewish custom? As the Jewish believers came together to discuss what to do, we see their decision-making process in Acts 15:28, *"For it seemed good to the Holy Spirit and to us."* There were no flashes of lightning from heaven or loud voice, there was just a sense that as they gathered and studied the scripture, prayed to seek the Lord, they came to a conclusion of what they should do.

3) Fasting

I find that fasting is one of the best tools to draw me closer to the heart of God. Fasting is not a way to twist God's arm into speaking to you about the direction you should go, but it is actually a way to put the desires of the flesh aside and say, "God, I am going to pursue you in this matter, and I am going to do it with intention." Start by fasting regularly once a week or even doing a three-day fast. Many books have been written on fasting, and much could be said on this topic; I will highlight a few. Fasting was and is a regular practice of believers, it is not just for those who are super spiritual; it is for everyday believers.

Acts 13:2-3: *"While they were worshiping the Lord and fasting, the Holy Spirit said, "Set apart for me Barnabas and Saul for the work to which I have called them." Then after fasting and praying, they laid their hands on them and sent them off."*

It is clear in this passage that worship and fasting were the primary drivers of breakthrough in seeking for direction.

If there is one practice that is neglected in hearing and discerning the will of God, I would say it is fasting. Fasting is not glamorous; it's hard, and can be discouraging. The apostles saw a breakthrough in a direction when they sought the Lord through prayer and fasting. This is a biblical precedent of how the church today should be operating; we must come back to the practice of fasting. In Acts chapter 9, both Saul and Annaias receive visions from the Lord while fasting about the direction they are to take. In seeking guidance from the Lord, fasting may be one of the greatest tools.

Prayer and fasting will be the catalyst for a great move of God. He desires to lead those who seek Him and unleash the plans and purposes for your life. Devote yourself to a life of fasting and prayer, and watch how God leads you into things only in your wildest dreams.

I love what Lou Engle says in his book, The Fast, "In fasting you break the gravitational pull of earthly things and set your mind on things above. You return to your first love. And sometimes, during and after the fast you slip the surly bonds of earth, dance the skies, tread the untrespassed sanctity of space and touch the face of God."[50]

I implore you to enter into fasting for the leading of Jesus in your life.

4) Confirmation

We must listen to the Lord for direction over time, especially when contemplating a major life transition. Ask the Lord to confirm what you are sensing and feeling with others. The Lord is so faithful and patient with us in this regard. He faithfully confirms His word through scripture, dreams, prophetic words, "random events" or "coincidences." The ways are endless in how the Lord confirms what He says through others. On multiple occasions, I have been spending time with the Lord in scripture, and then later that day, I will receive an email or text from a friend saying, I have been praying for you and am led to share this scripture with you. It ends up being the exact scripture I was meditating on! This is always so encouraging. First, it is encouraging because people are praying for me, and second, because God is speaking the same thing to them as He is to me.

I want to encourage you that God is concerned with decisions in your life, both large and small. There is no decision that is beyond Him. Becky and I had been married for three years, and we had been throwing around the idea of

---

[50] Lou Engle, The Fast (Colorado Springs: Engle House Publishing, 2020) 47

buying a house. This was a massive decision for me, and I hesitated in moving forward. We finally agreed that we would move forward in purchasing a home. We only had a little money and lived in a city with expensive housing. We began to take the steps to buying a home; we spoke with a realtor, mortgage broker and the bank. Our bank approved us for a large amount of money that we did not feel comfortable with spending. Becky and I asked the Lord for a maximum amount that we should spend on a house. We obeyed what the Lord said, and chose a home under the budget He gave to us. Over the years, we have spoken to each other multiple times about how grateful we are that we included the Lord in this huge decision and chose to walk in obedience to what He said.

I am always amazed and drawn to the story of Paul, Silas and Timothy in Acts.

Acts: 16:6-10: *"And they went through the region of Phrygia and Galatia, having been forbidden by the Holy Spirit to speak the word in Asia. And when they had come up to Mysia, they attempted to go into Bithynia, but the Spirit of Jesus did not allow them. So, passing by Mysia, they went down to Troas. And a vision appeared to Paul in the night: a man of Macedonia was standing there, urging him and saying, "Come over to Macedonia and help us." And when Paul had seen the vision, immediately we sought to go on into Macedonia, concluding that God had called us to preach the gospel to them."*

Paul was strategic where he felt like he was to go. I believe Paul was one of the most strategic missionaries we have ever

seen in Christianity. But even in his strategies, the Holy Spirit spoke to him, and he needed to adjust his plans. He was forbidden and redirected multiple times to where he was to go. CLOSED DOORS. The Lord opens and closes doors; sometimes, we believe that we are on the right track (and we are), and then the Lord redirects us. Occasionally, we know why, but most of the time, this side of heaven, we never find out. The Lord works in mysterious ways. What we can find peace and assurance in is that through it all, He is faithful to lead us in the next step. The scriptures are chalked full of the Lord leading His people. Isaiah 58:11 says,
"And the Lord will guide you continually and satisfy your desire in scorched places and make your bones strong; and you shall be like a watered garden, like a spring of water, whose waters do not fail."

Let us take comfort in the psalmist words in Psalm 48:14, *"This is God, our God forever and ever. He will guide us forever."* God can be trusted; He will never lead us astray; nothing surprises Him or is too great for Him to handle. Submit your ways to Him; I promise He will make your path straight. He will lead you beside quiet waters, and He will most certainly bring you into all that He has for you.

Prayer:

God, I thank you that you are the Good Shepherd and that your leadership is perfect. I thank you that I can trust you for direction in my life. You will speak and make your will known. You know all the days of my life, from beginning to end.

Activation:
1) Meditate on John 10:1-18.
2) Make plans to incorporate fasting into your rhythm of life. Start with trying a shorter fast. I highly encourage you to set aside one day a week to pray and fast. Longer fasts would include anywhere from three to forty days.
3) Lay before the Lord some large decisions you are thinking about; ask specific questions and journal what you sense He is saying. Share it with a trusted friend, mentor or leader, and ask for their input and prayer.

Chapter 10
Creating an Environment to Hear God's Voice

As we go on this journey of leaning into the voice of God, there are five primary conditions to hearing God's voice: humility, faith, a clean heart, a yielded will, and a willingness to wait.[51] Humility paves the way, faith makes it possible, a clean heart opens the door, a yielded will says yes to obedience, and waiting says "in your timing, God."

Walk in Humility

If we desire to walk in greater intimacy with the Lord and walk in all that He has for us, the number one thing that we must cultivate in our lives is an attitude of humility. Humility is the landing strip for the voice of God. Those who do not walk humbly will not take the time to inquire of God. We see this in the life of King Saul.

1 Chronicles 10:13-14: *"So Saul died for his breach of faith. He broke faith with the Lord in that he did not keep the command of the Lord, and also consulted a medium, seeking guidance. He did not seek guidance from the Lord. Therefore*

---

[51] Joy Dawson, Forever Ruined For the Ordinary, 17-22

the Lord put him to death and turned the kingdom over to David the son of Jesse."

Saul's lack of humility cost him his life. If we are going to hear from God, we have no other option but to walk in humility. The psalmist is confident that it is the humble who are led by God.

Psalm 25:9: *"He leads the humble in what is right and teaches the humble his way."*

Humility says, "I will wait on you." Pride says, "I can do it on my own." Jesus walked in immense humility and dependence upon the Father, and if we want to see a move of God we must walk with the same posture. The heart attitude of humility says, "Lord, we depend upon you for our very breath. Whether we need something small or large, we run to God first." James writes in his letter that God is for the humble, but he is against the proud (James 4:6).

Walk in Faith

All the heroes we look up to in the Bible walked with great faith; they believed in the promises of God and sought Him for their every need. When we come to the Lord, faith is required to seek and hear from Him. Like the writer of Hebrews shares, we must go to Him knowing that He desires to speak to us, to commune with us, and to reward those who seek Him with His voice. When we run to God in prayer for His leadership and guidance, we must believe that He wants to lead us and guide us. Will we believe and trust Him when He says, "I will guide you in all your steps?"

Isaiah 48:17: *"Thus says the Lord, your Redeemer, the Holy One of Israel: "I am the Lord your God, who teaches you to profit, who leads you in the way you should go."*

Walk in Purity of Heart

Psalm 66:18: *"If I had cherished iniquity in my heart, the Lord would not have listened."*

The Psalmist speaks to the reality of walking with a pure heart; if we have unconfessed sin in our hearts, it will prevent us from hearing God and the Lord not hearing our prayers. Unconfessed sin is one of the most significant barriers to not hearing God's voice. We usually don't need to dig too deep to know if we have unconfessed sin. It often sits close to the top of our minds and hearts; nagging at us until we deal with it. When we make unconfessed sin right, the burden lifts, and it's almost as if the heavens open up, and we begin to hear God again.

1 John 1:9: *"If we confess our sins, he is faithful and just to forgive us our sins and to cleanse us from all unrighteousness."*

When I have had unconfessed sin in my life, and I bring it to the light and make it right, the burden lifts, and I can hear God again. Until then, that is all I can think about. It consumes me. We must go before the Lord and have the heart attitude of the Psalmist that says *"search me O God."* We must walk in such a manner that we are asking the Lord to reveal anything in our lives that grieve Him.

A prayer that I have prayed many times is, "Lord, keep my heart soft towards you and your church." A soft heart towards God and others is crucial to living with a pure heart. I have seen far too many people get hurt, walk in unforgiveness, get angry at God, and leave the faith. This is heartbreaking. Scripture reminds us not to let bitterness take root; don't let it get a foothold in your life because it will wreak havoc.

Hebrews 12:15: *"See to it that no one fails to obtain the grace of God; that no "root of bitterness" springs up and causes trouble, and by it many become defiled."*
Ephesians:4:31: *"Let all bitterness and wrath and anger and clamor and slander be put away from you, along with all malice."*

Walk Yielded

Before Becky and I got married, we served in Youth With A Mission. We had very little money, but we desired to be used by God for His glory and plans and purposes. One day, we prayed together, and the Lord brought James 4:13-17 to Becky's mind. That day, we committed to the Lord to go wherever He would call us. This has been difficult at times, but as we have made Jesus the Lord of our lives, we have watched Him do incredible things.

James 4:13-17: *"Come now, you who say, "Today or tomorrow we will go into such and such a town and spend a year there and trade and make a profit"— yet you do not know what tomorrow will bring. What is your life? For you are a mist that appears for a little time and then vanishes. Instead* *you ought to say, "If the Lord wills, we will live and do this or that." As it is, you boast in your arrogance. All such boasting is evil. So whoever knows the right thing to do and fails to do it, for him it is sin."*

Many desire Jesus to be the Saviour of their lives, but few have given Christ Lordship. We desire to control our finances, our relationships, our careers and really, every aspect of our lives. This is not the call of Christ, but the call is to lay down everything at His feet. When we begin to yield to Him and His desires, the adventure begins. Do you desire to go on the most wild adventure with Jesus? If so, make Him the Lord of your life!

In 2008, I was in Thailand with a team of young missionaries. I was interested in dating a girl on the team (who is now my wife, Becky). I remember thinking one day, if I end up dating this girl and then marrying her, there is a very good chance I will move far away from where I grew up and from my family. This was difficult for me. I remember hearing the Lord so clearly, "Randall, forget the girl, are you willing to leave your city and family for me?" The fear of the Lord came upon me at that moment.

A life connected to Jesus, a life lived hearing His voice, is one that is yielded before Him. I implore you to not only know Jesus as your Saviour, but make Him your Lord.

Make Room and Wait

There are countless verses in the Bible about waiting upon God. Indeed, waiting is a vital characteristic of the Christian faith. We wait for promises to be fulfilled, for God to come through in our time of need, for the Lord to bring healing to those in need, and, most importantly, for the return of Christ. Waiting upon the Lord in prayer is one of the most challenging things to do as a believer, especially in a society with quick fixes and many distractions. The church must learn the discipline of waiting upon the Lord more than ever. We are always in a hurry. Sometimes, I find that I'm in a hurry going nowhere. The Lord is calling us to wait on Him. The Psalms are filled with this idea of waiting upon the Lord.

Psalm 27:14: *"Wait for the Lord; be strong, and let your heart take courage; wait for the Lord!"*
Psalm 130:5-6: *"I wait for the Lord, my soul waits, and in his word I hope; my soul waits for the Lord more than watchmen for the morning, more than watchmen for the morning."*

Psalm 62:5: *"For God alone, O my soul, wait in silence, for my hope is from him."*

If you are looking to God for the next step in your life, if you are looking for a breakthrough in ministry or your finances, if you need the Lord to come through in a significant way, I guarantee you that He will call you to wait upon Him. This is the biblical norm for any believer. One of my greatest weaknesses is being patient; this is not something I am proud of. How does the Lord work in impatient people? He makes them wait, not because He is mean, but because He is good.

Many spend time in prayer, bible reading, and worship, but how many have cultivated waiting upon the Lord? I suggest setting a timer on your phone. Start with five minutes in silence, fixing your gaze upon Jesus. The following week, set a ten-minute timer and begin to wait upon the Lord and hear His voice.

Prayer:

God, I desire to create an environment where I can hear your voice and walk in obedience. I humble myself before you and declare that I need you. Build my faith and trust in you as I walk on this journey of hearing your voice. I yield my will to you. I declare that you are my Lord. Search me, O God, and know me; try my thoughts and reveal anything that grieves your heart.

Activation:

Submit your deepest worries to God; finances, relationships, your calling, etc. Ask for His guidance and leadership in these areas. Ask Him what is your responsibility in each area, and what He wants to say to you. Create a daily routine of waiting on God in silence.

Chapter 11
Jesus and the Voice of God

John Wimber was a pastor, teacher, and founder of the Vineyard Movement. You may be familiar with the Vineyard; many of the worship songs that were sung in the late 70s, 80s and even into the 90s were written by John Wimber. In 1963, John gave his life to Christ after attending a Quaker bible study meeting and left his career as a professional musician with the "Righteous Brothers." One day, shortly after he gave his life to Christ, he had been reading through the gospels and studying the life of Jesus, and, along with his wife, Carol, had attended a church service. After the service, John asked the pastor, "So, when do we do the stuff?" "The 'stuff'," said the pastor. "What's the 'stuff'?" "You know," John replied, "the stuff in the Bible, like healing the sick and casting out demons. The stuff!" "Oh," replied the pastor. "We don't do the stuff. We believe they did it in biblical days, but we don't do it today." With a rather confused look on his face, John could only say, "And I gave up drugs for this?"[52]

---

[52] Sam Storms, Doin' the Stuff (Remembering John Wimber), Sam Storms, September 20,2023, www.samstorms.org/all-articles/post/doin-the-stuff---remembering-john-wimber--

Lord, save us from just knowing *about* you. We want to know you intimately and do everything you have called us to. Being a disciple of Jesus is more than just going to church on a Sunday, hearing a sermon, going to a Bible study on Wednesday and Thursday, or studying who Jesus is. Being a disciple of Jesus is also about doing the "stuff" that He did and taught us to do; it is about bringing the Kingdom of God to earth. Jesus exemplified with His life and teaching how we, as His followers, should live.

He tells His disciples that they will do greater works than He did.

John 14:12: *"Truly, truly, I say to you, whoever believes in me will also do the works that I do; and greater works than these will he do, because I am going to the Father."*

Jesus teaches His disciples that when He leaves, all those who considered themselves followers of Jesus would continue doing His work, and not only continue, but do it on a larger scale. Millions of Christians worldwide are continuing the work of Jesus and seeing incredible things happen!

Dr. Gordon Fee, a giant in the faith, in a lecture to YWAM students asked,

"Do you know what the foundational teaching of Jesus was? Love? Forgiveness? Many would go straight to these two teachings, and while they are essential and cannot be diminished, they were not the primary teachings of Christ. The number one teaching of Jesus is the Kingdom of God. Within the gospel writings of Matthew, Mark, Luke and John, the kingdom of God or Kingdom of heaven is referred to in ninety-two verses."[53]

The core teaching of Jesus is the Kingdom of God. Jesus not only taught about the Kingdom and what it looks like, but He also demonstrated what it looks like.

Mark 1:14-15: *"Jesus came into Galilee, proclaiming the gospel of God, and saying, "The time is fulfilled, and the kingdom of God is at hand; repent and believe in the gospel."*

If the primary teaching of Jesus was the Kingdom of God, one might ask, "well, what is the Kingdom of God?" John Wimber taught, "It is the rule of God in this present age, which has invaded the kingdom rule of satan, this present evil age. It is here in which signs and wonders occur. The rule of God was interrupted by the fall of man, which resulted in a state of rule by Satan and his armies. Jesus was sent to recover the fallen status. Essentially, Jesus came to right a wrong."[54]

We now live between the cross and the restoration of all things. It is a time we see the Kingdom of God breaking in. Many have called it the "now but not yet," where God's Kingdom hasn't been realized in all its fullness. In this time, we still endure death, pain, sorrow, grieving, sadness and a whole

---

[53] Gordon Fee, The Kingdom of God, Youtube Video, 100:07, June 30, 2014 youtu.be/qV0jqooBA6w?si=0CxTB4cj0OP1y4gO

[54] John Wimber, The Kingdom of God, Youtube Video, 8:39, September 4th, 2010, youtu.be/ei60RPRWVCE?si=RvVeYeH84YMN6p3C

host of difficult things, but when Jesus comes again (His second coming), we will see the restoration of all things.

Timeline of History and Future Events
1) Creation (Genesis 1)
2) The Garden (Genesis 2)
3) The Fall of Man (Genesis 3)
4) The Cross (Matthew 27, Mark 15, Luke 23, John 19)
5) The Resurrection (Matthew 28, Mark 16, Luke 24, John 20)
   - *The period in which we live.*
6) The Restoration of all things (Revelation 21)

Not only did Jesus teach *about* the kingdom of God, but He also *demonstrated* it. Thus, many have called Jesus' ministry a proclamation and a demonstration of the Kingdom of God. Jesus used words to teach and miraculous works to demonstrate.

In Luke 4, after Jesus has just called His first disciples, He goes immediately into the temple and begins to teach. Interestingly enough, He pulls the scroll and begins to read Isaiah 61, a portion of scripture referring to the Kingdom of God and the Good News. Within a few moments, a demonic spirit manifests, and Jesus silences it and casts it out. In this moment, we see Jesus proclaiming and demonstrating the Kingdom of God.

Luke 4:17-19: *"And the scroll of the prophet Isaiah was given to him. He unrolled the scroll and found the place where it was written, "The Spirit of the Lord is upon me, because he has anointed me to proclaim good news to the poor. He has sent me* *to proclaim liberty to the captives and recovering of sight to the blind, to set at liberty those who are oppressed, to proclaim the year of the Lord's favour."*

I believe that if we are to be the church that Jesus desires us to be, we will proclaim the good news *and* demonstrate the good news; we will be the vehicle by which the Kingdom of God is released. That means, you and I, empowered by the Spirit, are called to do the things that Jesus did. We are to pray the way Jesus taught the disciples, and live in such a way that we bring the Kingdom of God, the realities of heaven to earth, through the power of the Holy Spirit, in the name of Jesus.

Power and Authority

Within a kingdom, or even area of society, there are levels of power and authority. Jesus has given us power and authority to release the Kingdom of God wherever we go. Luke and Matthew both record the words of Jesus in this regard.

Luke 9:1-2: *"And he called the twelve together and gave them power and authority over all demons and to cure diseases, and he sent them out to proclaim the kingdom of God and to heal."*

Matthew 10:1: *"And he called to him his twelve disciples and gave them authority over unclean spirits, to cast them out, and to heal every disease and every affliction."*

Jesus has given **power** and **authority** over every disease and affliction, and every demonic force to those who follow Him and believe in His name. Webster's dictionary defines the word power as "the ability, the strength and the might to complete a given task."[55] The word "power" in the Greek language means "dunamis,"[56] which is where we get our word dynamite. We have been given dynamite power, not just any power. Webster's dictionary defines the word authority as "the power to influence or command."[57] The word authority in the original language is a Greek word, "exousia,"[58] which means "the right to control or govern, dominion, the area or sphere of jurisdiction."

In crime movies, you will often see a crime committed, and two police jurisdictions will show up; one jurisdiction will say to the other, "You have no right to be here. You have no jurisdiction. This is our crime scene." In the Kingdom of God, Jesus has given His followers jurisdiction over all sickness, disease, and the demonically oppressed; He has given us power and authority to set the wrong things right. He has given us power and authority over the enemy.

Recently, I was invited to speak at a weekend retreat for a church. At the end of one of the sessions, I wanted to have a time of ministry where people could be prayed for. I called the

---

[55] "Power" *Merriam-Webster.com.* October 14, 2023, merriam-webster.com/dictionary/power, September, 25,2023

[56] Strong's #1411, Bible Tools, Church of the Great God, September 14,2023, www.bibletools.org/index.cfm/fuseaction/Lexicon.show/ID/G1411/dunamis.htm

[57] "Authority," *Merriam-Webster.com.* October 17,2023, merriam-webster.com/dictionary/authority, September 25th, 2023

[58] Strong's #1849, Bible Tools, Church of the Great God, September 14,2023, www.bibletools.org/index.cfm/fuseaction/Lexicon.show/ID/G1849/exousia.htm

leaders to the front, and asked people to come forward for ministry as they felt led. At one point, a guy approached me, and I prayed with him. He wanted to talk about a few things, so I went with another leader to the back of the room to talk. Ten minutes later, one of the leaders came running over to me and said, "Randall, you're going to want to come here!" So, I finished up with the guy and walked over. There were about 4-5 people huddled around a young lady. She was crying, and she began to tell me how she had been in a car accident ten years prior, causing a back injury that wouldn't go away. She had been to doctors and chiropractors and had many treatments, but nothing worked. While a couple of the leaders were praying over her, she felt muscles in her upper back and shoulder move and shift, and her pain had completely dissipated! The leaders exercised the authority and power they had been given to release healing over her back. Praise God for His wonderful work!

The Mandate of Jesus

Jesus had a mandate on His life and He revealed it in His very first sermon as He came out of the wilderness in the power of the Holy Spirit. Jesus went into the temple and declared,

Luke 4:18: *"The Spirit of the Lord is upon me, because he has anointed me to proclaim good news to the poor. He has sent me to proclaim liberty to the captives and recovering of sight to the blind, to set at liberty those who are oppressed."*

Jesus is quoting Isaiah 61, which is the good news in demonstration, destroying the works of the devil, going to the cross to break the power of sin and death. The mandate of Jesus is now our mandate. We have been anointed with power from on high to free captives, break the chains in Jesus' name, give sight to the blind, and to free the oppressed. We are called to release the Kingdom of God on earth. Hearing the voice of God is crucial to this mandate; we must follow the guiding and leading of the Holy Spirit to walk this out.

How did Jesus Minister?

Jesus lived a life dependent on the Father through the power of the Holy Spirit. Read that again. Jesus lived a life dependent on the Father through the power of the Holy Spirit. Philippians 2:1-11 is one of the most profound passages of scripture in relation to how Jesus lived and operated while on earth.

Philippians 2:5-8: *"Have this mind among yourselves, which is yours in Christ Jesus, **who, though he was in the form of God, did not count equality with God a thing to be grasped, but emptied himself, by taking the form of a servant, being born in the likeness of men. And being found in human form, he humbled himself by becoming obedient to the point of death, even death on a cross.**"*

Jesus was, is and will always be one hundred percent God; while He was on earth, He chose to limit Himself to live as a human fully dependent on the Holy Spirit. This is extremely important. Jesus never played the "God card" so He could do whatever He wanted; He subjected Himself to living fully human, dependent upon the Father through the power of the Holy Spirit (while still being one hundred percent God). When Jesus lived on earth he was never less than God but he lived as though he was never more than a man. Jesus as a man needed to wait upon and rely on the Holy Spirit in order to minister to people. Jesus in doing so, gave us the model for every single follower of Jesus.

Hebrews 2:17: *"Therefore he had to be made like his brothers in every respect, so that he might become a merciful and faithful high priest in the service of God, to make propitiation for the sins of the people."*
Hebrews 4:15: *"For we do not have a high priest who is unable to sympathize with our weaknesses, but one who in every respect has been tempted as we are, yet without sin."*

Some have asked why Jesus needed to be baptized if He was completely sinless (which He was). Jesus needed to be baptized to give His followers an example and receive the anointing of the Holy Spirit. When Jesus came out of the water, the Holy Spirit descended upon Him in the form of a dove. Luke 3:22 says, *"and the Holy Spirit descended on him in bodily form, like a dove."* Jesus *needed* the empowerment of the Spirit. Jesus lived on this earth one hundred percent God and one hundred percent man. He performed miracles, cast out demons, healed the sick and raised the dead as a man, fully dependent upon the Spirit. He did this so He could be our perfect example of a life lived dependent upon the Father through the empowerment of the Spirit.

Acts 10:38: *"How God anointed Jesus of Nazareth with the Holy Spirit and with power. He went about doing good and healing all who were oppressed by the devil, for God was with him."*

This may be a significant step theologically for some of you, which is understandable. Many of us have grown up and never understand that Jesus lived the life He did by living surrendered to the Spirit. It is interesting that we are okay with looking to Jesus in every area of life as our example (love, forgiveness, holy living), except we are not when it comes to the ways of the miraculous. I do not deny the divinity of Jesus for a second; even while Jesus was on earth, He was one hundred percent divine; however, if Jesus played the God card, not living as a human entirely dependent upon the Father in the power of the Holy Spirit, how could He be our example? How could Jesus say that we would do even greater works than He did? We would never be able to ask, "What would Jesus do?" in a certain situation, because it would be entirely out of the realm of possibility. What do we then make of the words of Christ throughout the gospels?

Mark 16:17-18: *"And these signs will accompany those who believe: in my name they will cast out demons; they will speak in new tongues; they will pick up serpents with their hands; and if they drink any deadly poison, it will not hurt them; they will lay their hands on the sick, and they will recover."*

Jesus Dependant upon the Father Through the Spirit

The Christian journey is not one of trying harder, doing more or being better, but a message of surrender and dependence. I cannot walk in the things Jesus has called us to in His word just by trying harder. Most of us have tried this many times and continually fail. Many of us have besetting sins we can't overcome and walk in victory. Most of us have habits that are either sinful or destructive. The key is not to try, try, try and try some more; the key is to die. Yes, you read that right, die.

Galatians 2:20: *"I have been crucified with Christ. It is no longer I who live, but Christ who lives in me. And the life I now live in the flesh, I live by faith in the Son of God, who loved me and gave himself for me."*

We walk in freedom from a life of destruction by living dependent upon the Spirit. Every morning, we must wake up and surrender to the Holy Spirit. We must die to ourselves. For many, worry is a common struggle. There are many unknowns and fears, some of which are valid. Worry, however, doesn't help anyone. A few years ago, the Holy Spirit was working on some of the worries I struggled with, and I realized I needed His help if I was going to walk in victory. I would lay in my bed, release the worry to Him, and then I would pray, "Holy Spirit, would you produce the fruit of peace in my life, because when I try to produce peace, it comes out as fear (Galatians 5:22-23)." I couldn't produce peace in my life by trying harder or trying to "just stop worrying," but the Spirit of God could produce peace in me. As I surrendered to Him, He brought about a life filled with peace. Jesus was our perfect example of dependency on the Spirit. He became our perfect example of walking in love, sacrifice, and walking victorious over sin (even though on this side of heaven, we will never be perfect or sinless). He became our perfect example of walking in the miraculous, healing and the things of the Spirit; an example of being dependent upon the voice of His Father in heaven. Jesus lived a life dependent upon the Father throughout His entire earthly ministry. Hundreds of years before Jesus came to earth, Isaiah prophesied about Jesus. He said that Jesus would hear the words of the Father and be taught by Him.

Isaiah 50:4: *"Morning by morning he awakens; he awakens my ear to hear as those who are taught."*

Jesus did everything from a foundation of hearing and seeing what the Father said. His life was filled with moments where He slipped away from the crowds, the noise and the busyness of life to connect with the Father. There was no other option. How different would our lives look if we woke up every morning and the first words we heard were from our Father in heaven? What if we were taught by the Father every morning, being affirmed in our identity as sons and daughters, rather than being berated by the voices of social media?

Mark 1:35: *"And rising very early in the morning, while it was still dark, he departed and went out to a desolate place, and there he prayed."*

The first thing we do in our day will set the trajectory of our day. It is very easy for me to wake up, roll over and spend fifteen minutes on my phone before I even get out of bed. Jesus sets the tone of His day by connecting with the Father before it is even light enough to see. He makes sure the connection lines are open and that He can hear the voice of His Father.

Jesus Dependent on the Voice of God

Jesus performed many miracles and healings; He gave prophetic words, words of knowledge and wisdom, and walked in incredible discernment, among many other things. In John 5:19, Jesus gives us insight into how He operated in His ministry while on earth.

John 5:19: *"So Jesus said to them, "Truly, truly, I say to you, the Son can do nothing of his own accord, but only what he sees the Father doing. For whatever the Father does, that the Son does likewise."*

I believe everything in Jesus' life came from a heart attitude of leaning into the voice of His father at all times; how He responded to the Pharisees and leaders of the day, how He related to the disciples, and how He loved the outcast. In John 8:28-29 Jesus also states that He does nothing on His own accord, but He speaks only what the Father has taught Him; a life dependent on the voice of His Father. This is a great challenge for us today. There are so many things that can take up our time; there are so many causes and ministries, and yet we must only do what we hear the Spirit saying to us. What is Jesus saying to you? How does this translate into our businesses and being Kingdom-minded? As a Kingdom minded business or politician, how is Jesus asking you to release the kingdom on earth, to bind up the brokenhearted? How does it translate into parenting and raising our kids? What about our marriages and relationships? What if a whole generation of parents prophesied over their children? What if parents would call out the prophetic destinies in their kids and their kids knew who they were created to be, rather than stumbling through their teens and into their twenties and thirties? The world would be a very different place. What if we did only the things that Jesus said to do in our businesses, even though some ideas might be completely different from what the world would do? What if in our parenting, we were Spirit-led and prayed about schools, movies, friends, and all the other activities? What if when our kids were having meltdowns, instead of yelling at them and getting frustrated, we went to the Holy Spirit and said, "lead me; I need help?" Our lives would look completely different.

      One day, when our oldest daughter was about four years old, she was speaking rudely to Becky while we were sitting in the car in the driveway of our house. At one point, I looked calmly at Olivia and said, "Olivia, could you take a moment and ask Jesus how He wants you to speak to your mother?" About ten seconds later, she began apologizing to Becky for the way she was speaking to her. Could this be a new way of parenting, by the power of the Spirit? What if we lived every aspect of our life with this in mind? What if you work from home and find different places in your community to work, such as a coffee shop, restaurant, library, or community workspace so that you could release the Kingdom of God in your city or town? What if every day when you woke up, you got ready to leave the house and said, "Holy Spirit, where do you want me to work today?" Some of you are saying, "Randall, come on; certainly, God doesn't care about the location of where I work today." What if the Lord has a divine assignment for you at the local coffee shop, but you never cared to ask where you should work and missed out on what He had for you that day? Now, I don't want you to worry about missing out on what God has for you, but I want you to think about living a life led by the Spirit. We want to be the hands and feet of Jesus, but if we aren't going where He is leading, then what are we doing? The Spirit speaks in all areas of our lives; are we listening? Are we only doing what we see the Father doing?

Jesus Dependent in Prayer

Throughout the gospels, specifically Luke, the authors were attentive to the details of Jesus' life. One of those details was the life of prayer that Jesus exemplified. There were many instances where Jesus spent time in a quiet place or a place where no one else was around, and even spent an entire night in prayer, listening to His Father, asking the Father to lead Him and guide Him in all that He did.

Here are a few examples from the gospel of Luke:

Luke 4:42: *"And when it was day, he departed and went into a desolate place"*
Luke 5:16: *"But he would withdraw to desolate places and pray."*

Luke 6:12: *"In these days he went out to the mountain to pray, and all night he continued in prayer to God."*

The results of Jesus' prayer life were many; when the disciples could not cast out a demon, Jesus told them that this kind only comes out through prayer and fasting. The primary result of Jesus' prayer life, was that He was connected to the Father. He listened to His Father's voice before any other voices. How many times in prayer did the Father affirm His identity? How many times in prayer did the Father show Him what He must do? How many times in prayer did He hear the voice of His Father telling Him how to lead the disciples and connect with each one of them? Again, the words of Jesus ring loudly about His dependence on the Father.

John 5:30: *"I can do nothing on my own. As I hear, I judge, and my judgment is just, because I seek not my own will but the will of him who sent me."*

Prophetic Evangelism

Evangelism has become somewhat of a taboo word in our culture; it is so bad that, according to Barna in 2019, almost half of Christians believed that evangelism was wrong.[59] Today, the sentiment towards evangelism has not changed. Maybe the picture these Christians have in mind is a man or woman standing on the corner of the street yelling something

---

[59] Barna, "Almost Half of Practicing Christian Millennials Say Evangelism Is Wrong," Barna, Barna, September 10, 2023, www.barna.com/research/millennials-oppose-evangelism/

about burning in hell. Jesus is the only one who can give life and life abundantly. Therefore, I am obligated to tell the world about the person of Jesus and what He has done in my life and desires to do for others. I am obligated to release the kingdom of God wherever I go. Ultimately, we want to see the world come to know Jesus, their lives radically changed, and the powers of darkness be destroyed.

1 John 3:8: *"The reason the Son of God appeared was to destroy the works of the devil."*

Jesus sends out His disciples and tells them to proclaim and demonstrate the good news. This is not about getting people to say the "sinners prayer," this is about proclaiming the Kingdom of God and demonstrating the realities of it.

If we have the Spirit of God in us and moving through us, we are walking in the power of the Holy Spirit just like the early believers; we are walking encounters. What I mean by this is that the Holy Spirit doesn't just want to stay inside of us, but ever since we have been baptized in the Spirit, He wants to get out! He desires to encounter others through our obedience. He desires to draw everyone to Jesus (John 16:13-14).

1 Corinthians 4:20: *"For the kingdom of God does not consist in talk but in power."*

People need to know they are not just conforming to a system of thinking, but encountering a living God. This happens when we listen to the voice of God for other people and share it with them, or when we hear what Jesus is saying and step out in faith to accomplish it. Some have called this a power encounter. When the Spirit of God reveals things about others, it brings their defenses down and opens up a doorway to share the goodness and love of Jesus Christ. It shows that Jesus cares about the details of our lives and isn't an angry God. Man-made arguments and discussion have their place, but they can only go so far; I believe that Jesus sets the precedent for prophetic evangelism when He meets the woman at the well (John 4). The conversation starts with Jesus asking for some water, but goes deep quickly. Jesus has a word of knowledge about the woman's past. This word of knowledge brings her defenses down and allows Jesus to get to the heart of the matter. Not only this, but it shows the woman how deeply God cares about her, the details of her life and her struggles. He knows her intimately before she even knows Him. If we are to model ourselves after Jesus, then throughout our day, we need to be asking, "Father, what are you doing? Jesus, how do you want me to minister in this situation? Jesus, do you want to heal someone today? Jesus, how can I partner with what you are already doing?" Jesus has an assignment for us to release the Kingdom of God on earth every single day.

I was at the gym one time and saw this gentleman, probably in his forties, along with two teenagers. I felt like I was to minister to him, so I began to pray for the man in my thoughts. The Lord showed me that this man had the gift of leadership on his life, and that if he gave his life to Jesus, he would be used in a mighty way. I kept praying for him; I knew I was supposed to go over and talk with him, but I was too chicken; I didn't have the boldness to share with him. To this day, I know that word was from the Lord. There are times when we walk in obedience, and there are times when we fail. The first thing we need to know is that there is grace. The Lord is not condemning us for times we missed it, but He offers grace to step out of the boat next time.

We live in a city of 1.6 million people. We love this city and believe God has called us here. In a large city like this, it is rare to run into people you know on a day-to-day basis. During a short period of time (roughly a month or two), we ran into one of Becky's childhood friends three times. This friend is not a believer and, in fact, really wanted nothing to do with God. After running into her three times, in three separate areas of the city, the Lord had got my attention. While talking with her in the middle of a mall, I began to pray for her in my head. As I prayed, I asked the Holy Spirit what He wanted to say to her. I felt like the Lord said, "Tell her I love her, and I have not forgotten her; she is special to me." When there was a pause in the conversation, I told her what the Lord was saying. She smiled and thanked me, and that was the end of the conversation. There wasn't much else to it. She didn't give her life to Jesus at that moment, but it undoubtedly got her thinking.

Not every time we step out in obedience will someone give their life to Jesus, even though this is certainly our hope. At times, there may be some opposition to the message that we carry. I believe we must have a different mindset. As we share the love of Jesus with those around us, and see the invading of the Kingdom of God, some of us will plant seeds, while others will water the seeds. God is the one who makes them grow, and the Holy Spirit is the one who is awakening hearts to the reality of new life in Jesus (1 Corinthians 3:6-9). Have you been obedient to what the Lord is asking of you?

A few years ago, I was filling my car up with gas. A gentleman walked up to me with a gas can and said, "Hey I need some gas for my car, but don't have any money. Would you mind filling up this gas can?" I replied, "Yes, absolutely, however I want you to know something first. Jesus loves you and desires to be in a relationship with you; you have not been forgotten." He looked at me, took the chain necklace from around his neck and showed it to me. "Look, man, my Grandma gave me this necklace, and she prays for me all the time." This gentleman, although he did not give his life to Jesus, encountered God through an act of kindness and through a realization that God was pursuing him. The prayers of his Grandma were paying off!

First, We Wait!

Before we go out and do "the stuff," we must wait upon the Lord. Moments before Jesus ascended into heaven, He gave his disciples strict instructions to wait in Jerusalem for the promise of the Father, the Holy Spirit!

Acts 1:4-5: *And while staying with them he ordered them not to depart from Jerusalem, but to wait for the promise of the Father, which, he said, "you heard from me; for John baptized with water, but you will be baptized with the Holy Spirit not many days from now."*

Jesus knew and exemplified that apart from the Holy Spirit, the disciples would be powerless. If they were going to do "greater things," they were not going to be able to do it on their own, they needed the empowering presence of the Holy Spirit.

Acts 1:8: *But you will receive power when the Holy Spirit has come upon you, and you will be my witnesses in Jerusalem and in all Judea and Samaria, and to the end of the earth."*

Just like the disciples and believers in the first century, we too, must be baptized and empowered by the Holy Spirit. To be brutally honest, the Holy Spirit is our only hope in fulfilling the mandate to make disciples of all nations. A.W. Tozer said, "The Spirit-filled life is not a special deluxe edition of Christianity. It is part and parcel of the total plan of God for His people."[60]

Mark 16:15-18: *And he said to them, "Go into all the world and proclaim the gospel to the whole creation. Whoever believes and is baptized will be saved, but whoever does not believe will be condemned. And these signs will accompany those who believe: in my name they will cast out demons; they will speak in new tongues; they will pick up serpents with their hands; and if they drink any deadly poison, it will not hurt them; they will lay their hands on the sick, and they will recover."*

---

[60] A.W. Tozer, How to Be Filled with the Holy Spirit (Louisville, Kentucky: GLH Publishing, 1952) 20

I implore you to wait! How long? Until you know you have been filled! When the Holy Spirit fills us, there is evidence that He has come. It might be unsurpassable peace, it might be tears and weeping, it might even be like a mighty rushing wind!

Acts 2:1-4: *When the day of Pentecost arrived, they were all together in one place. 2 And suddenly there came from heaven a sound like a mighty rushing wind, and it filled the entire house where they were sitting. 3 And divided tongues as of fire appeared to them and rested on each one of them. 4 And they were all filled with the Holy Spirit and began to speak in other tongues as the Spirit gave them utterance.*

Prayer:

Jesus, I need your Spirit! Come and fill me to a place of overflowing today! Thank you for calling me to hear your voice in everything I do. You care about the "little" and "big" things. Help me yield to your voice today as I go to the grocery store, get my kids ready for school, go to the bank, or fill my vehicle with gas. You are always with me.

Activation:

1) Spend time waiting upon the Lord for Him to baptize you with His Spirit, to empower you to do mighty works and live a life pleasing to Him. (See Appendix*)

2) Choose an area of your life: work, school, home, children, marriage, or family.

Just like Jesus, we are called to proclaim and demonstrate the kingdom of God on earth. As you think through this list, ask the Lord to highlight an area you feel you are to release the kingdom of God into. If it's your children, begin praying for each of them and ask the Lord for a word and share it with them. Speak destiny over them. Ask the Lord for an encouraging word for a co-worker or the teller at the bank. As you listen to His voice, He may ask you to prophesy over someone or ask you to serve someone; whatever it is, be obedient to His voice and watch as the kingdom of God is released in your midst.

Chapter 12: Conclusion
The Extraordinary Journey

Ephesians 3:14-21: *"For this reason I bow my knees before the Father, from whom every family in heaven and on earth is named, that according to the riches of his glory he may grant you to be strengthened with power through his Spirit in your inner being, so that Christ may dwell in your hearts through faith—that you, being rooted and grounded in love, may have strength to comprehend with all the saints what is the breadth and length and height and depth, and to know the love of Christ that surpasses knowledge, that you may be filled with all the fullness of God. Now to him who is able to do far more abundantly than all that we ask or think, according to the power at work within us, to him be glory in the church and in Christ Jesus throughout all generations, forever and ever. Amen."*

I want to close this book the same way that I began, with a word of encouragement; there is more! There is more to God than you are currently experiencing. He has more to give than you can possibly know. I once heard someone say, "You have as much of God as you want." I so desire that you would press into hearing God's voice, as it will radically change your life. The Puritan, Charles Hodge wrote, "The indwelling Christ is a thing of degrees."[61] Meaning we can have more or less of God flowing in our lives. God will never withhold Himself from you, so press into Him. The journey that you are on with the Lord was never intended to be boring, it was never intended to be lifeless and mundane; we serve a God who is able to do far more abundantly than all we can ask or think. Wow, how incredible!

Don't settle for anything less than all that God has for you. Don't settle for a faithless Christianity. Don't give into fear that tells you, "if you cannot accumulate the things of this world, you will be unfulfilled." Having a bigger house, a fancier car, a six-figure job and all the things of this world will not make you happy. You will be the most fulfilled in walking completely surrendered to the Holy Spirit.

In Paul's letter to the Ephesian church, he shares some of the most brilliant theological insights in the first three chapters. He writes that we have been given every spiritual blessing in Christ, that we have been adopted as sons and daughters, that we are chosen in Christ before the foundations of the world to be holy and blameless, that we have redemption by His blood, that we have forgiveness of our trespasses, and that we have been sealed by the promised Holy Spirit among many other things. Paul gets to the middle of his letter and he stops and begins to pray for the believers. He doesn't just want the church to "know" in their head these wonderful theological

---

[61] John Stott, The Message of Ephesians. (Downers Grove, IL: Intervarsity Press, 1984)

truths, but he desires that they would come to "know" them in their hearts, and that they would experience them and encounter a living God.

Theologian, John Stott, refers to Paul's famous prayer as a "staircase prayer that keeps going higher and higher."[62] In this prayer there are four steps;

1) That the believers would be strengthened with power
2) That they would be rooted and grounded in love
3) That they would know the love of Christ that surpasses understanding
4) That they would be filled with all the fullness of God

At the foundation of his prayer is this beautiful phrase, "According to the riches of His glory." Paul prays *according* to the riches of God's glory. What does this mean? I think, in part, it means we have a God who gives without holding back; some poets and songwriters have called it "reckless." It's over-the-top, never stopping, lavish giving. He is a well that never runs dry. There is always MORE in Christ; more love, more patience, more kindness, more awe, more wonder, more joy, more peace. He is an endless ocean and a bottomless sea. Paul's earnest desire is that the church would experience these realities and that they would experience all that God has for them in Christ. Paul approaches the Father in prayer, according to His immeasurable greatness, His incredible acts, immeasurable goodness, His limitless power, His incredible

---

[62] John Stott, The Message of Ephesians.

splendor and brilliance, and His limitless resources; the very character and nature of who God is.

I love how Eugene Peterson writes it in the Message Bible, "I pray to the Father who parcels out all of heaven!" Wow! Paul prays from a place of knowing that in Christ there is more for him and the Christians in Ephesus.

Strengthened with Power

In Paul's earnest prayer we see his deep desire that the believers would be strengthened with power in their inner being ("strengthened with might.") In the previous chapter, I mentioned Jesus gave us power and authority. The same word "dunamis" (power) is used by Paul in this context. Paul asks that the church would be strengthened with dynamite power in their inner being. In 1867 Alfred Nobel created an explosive and coined it "dynamite"[63] because of its incredible power. Dynamite completely changed the landscape of global industrialization because it was so powerful that it could blow through mountains and other land masses to build tunnels, canals, and then further build railway tracks and roads. Paul's desire is that we would be strengthened with not just any power but *dynamite* power.

We all need to be strengthened. Every new year, many make resolutions to go to the gym and strengthen themselves. While many fail at these resolutions, we cannot afford to fail at being strengthened in our inner being. We go through many challenges in life: unexpected deaths, disappointments,

---

[63] Erik Gregersen, Alfred Nobel, Britannica, November 28, 2023, www.britannica.com/biography/Alfred-Nobel, 2023

failures, financial crisis, job loss and the list goes on. We must be strengthened with dynamite power.

How can we be strengthened with this dynamite power, you ask? Paul quickly answers this question, "through His Spirit in your inner being." The Holy Spirit is the one who will strengthen us with power; He lives in us and dwells in us.

Romans 8:11: *"If the Spirit of him who raised Jesus from the dead dwells in you, he who raised Christ Jesus from the dead will also give life to your mortal bodies through his Spirit who dwells in you."*
1 Corinthians 6:19: *"Or do you not know that your body is a temple of the Holy Spirit within you, whom you have from God?"*

Take a moment right where you are, put your hand on your chest and say, "The Holy Spirit dwells in me." Many will try to strengthen their inner being by doing yoga or meditations, or trying to empty themselves. As far as I'm concerned, I'll take the Holy Spirit! I'll take the Spirit who raised Jesus from the dead to strengthen my inner being. It is the continual assumption of the New Testament writers that the strength in the Christian life comes from the personal indwelling of the Spirit of Christ.

Why do we need to be strengthened? We need to be strengthened so that Christ can have more of us, so that Christ can dwell in our hearts through faith, and so that we can receive all that God has for us, the "more" that is in Christ Jesus. Paul's prayer is that the Holy Spirit would intervene and build us up so that Christ might dwell in us to a greater capacity, that Christ would make His home in our hearts. The Spirit of Christ is not looking to rent a room for a night or two, but He is looking to take up permanent residency, and expand the borders of our heart so that Christ can take His rightful place, on the throne of our hearts.

As you go on this incredible journey of listening to God, remember that Christ is looking to possess you in a greater capacity, His life infiltrating your life, a life that is completely surrendered to His plans and purposes. There is indeed more for you.

Rooted and Grounded

Paul prays that the Ephesian church would be rooted and grounded in love. Our love for one another should be at the forefront of our lives. The natural outworking of the Spirit filled life, with Christ seated on the throne of our heart, is love for one another. Being rooted and grounded both have connotations of a tree and a foundation. The roots of a tree make it unshakeable, and the foundation of a house or building will similarly do the same. Jesus states;

John 13:35: *"By this everyone will know that you are my disciples, if you love one another."*

Our love for one another will prove that we are of Christ. As we listen to His voice, as we walk in the gifts of the Spirit to build up the church, let us love one another. Let us be rooted and grounded in our love for the body of Christ, for the world around us that desperately needs Jesus. There is more love that

Jesus wants to pour out through us as He guides us and leads us.

Knowledge of the Love of Christ

The third step in Paul's staircase prayer is that the believers would have the strength to comprehend with all the saints what is the breadth, length, height and depth of the love of Christ for all believers. He desires the believers to know the love of Christ that surpasses all knowledge.

As F.F. Bruce comments on the love of God in his commentary on Ephesians, he compares the wisdom of God with the love of God.[64] Bruce points to Job 11:8-9 speaking of God's wisdom to best describe God's love.

Job 11:8-9: *"It is higher than heaven—what can you do? Deeper than Sheol—what can you know? Its measure is longer than the earth and broader than the sea."*

If the wisdom of God is higher than heaven and deeper than Sheol, and it measures longer than the earth and broader than the sea, then the love of God is unsearchable and unfathomable. The human mind simply cannot comprehend the love of God. How do we know the love of Christ that surpasses knowledge? We must encounter God Himself.

The Spirit within us, connects us to the love of Christ, that we might experience
His love. Pauls says in his letter to the Corinthians;

---

[64] F.F. Bruce, NICNT Ephesians (Grand Rapids, Michigan: WM. B. Eerdmans Publishing, 1984)78-85

1 Corinthians 2:10: *"These things God has revealed to us through the Spirit. For the Spirit searches everything, even the depths of God."*

The Spirit searches all things so that we might cry out with our spirits "Abba Father."

Romans 8:15-16: *"For you did not receive the spirit of slavery to fall back into fear, but you have received the Spirit of adoption as sons, by whom we cry, "Abba! Father!" The Spirit himself bears witness with our spirit that we are children of God."*

The only way to know something that is unknowable, is to *experience* it, to encounter it. Oh that we would "know" the unknowable love of God! I echo the words of Charles Spurgeon, "In this measurement may you and I be skilled. If we know nothing of mathematics, may we be well-tutored scholars in this spiritual geometry, and be able to comprehend the breaths and lengths of Jesus' precious love."[65]

We are so good in the Western world when it comes to "knowledge," and it has crept into the church. We have Master's degrees, Doctorate degrees, and we are educated until we are blue-in-the-face, yet many of us don't "know" the love

---

[65] David Guzek, EPHESIANS 3 – THE REVEALING OF GOD'S MYSTERY, Enduring Word Bible Commentary, November 28, 2023enduringword.com/bible-commentary/ephesians-3/

of God that surpasses knowledge. We are so good at "knowing" about God, yet we lack encounter with Him. As we listen to His voice, let us daily encounter a living God, let the words of Jesus wash over us, "you are my son or daughter with whom I am well pleased."

All the Fullness of God

Paul's prayer summits with a desire to be filled with "all the fullness of God." Can you imagine? **All** the fullness of God! Certainly we have not even scratched the surface of who God is, and yet Paul prays that we might be filled with "ALL" the fullness of God. Can I say it again? There is more in Christ, there is more of His goodness to experience.

Colossians 2:9: *"For in him the whole fullness of deity dwells bodily."*

Far More Abundantly

Paul closes his prayer with one of the most beautiful sentences.

Ephesians 3:20: *"Now to Him who is able to do far more abundantly than all that we ask or think, according to the power at work within us."*

Some have stated that Paul had to invent a new phrase in order to describe what God is able to do. "Exceedingly abundantly more" than all we ask or think. What God can actually do exceeds abundance. We often think far too small for how God can work in and through us, but it's time to start thinking bigger. God is able! Think of the largest thing you have ever asked God; He is able to do more than that! Maybe there is something that you want to ask God, but you're a little scared that it's too big. *More than that!*

Some of you are not sure whether you want more. You question, "What will it cost me?" Friendships? Reputation? Finances? Community? What will happen if I fully surrender to the Holy Spirit and all that God has for me? Let me remind you that He is the Good Shepherd, and all that He has for you and does in you is for your good.

It is time to break out of the box of who you think God to be, and dive into the journey of listening to His voice. He has far more for your life than you ever think or imagine!

Prayer: God, I thank you that in Jesus there is more. I ask that as I learn to hear your voice, You would lead me into all that you have for me. I thank you that I could never plumb the depths of who you are.

Activation: Put your hand on your chest and say, "Holy Spirit, fill me with all the fullness of God. I want all that you have for me."

Prophetic Act: Stand up and take a few steps forward and with your mouth declare, "I step into **all** that God has for me."

Appendix
How to Be Filled with the Holy Spirit

The Prophet Joel proclaimed that God would one day pour out His Spirit on all flesh.

Joel 2:28-29: *"And it shall come to pass afterward, that I will pour out my Spirit on all flesh; your sons and your daughters shall prophesy, your old men shall dream dreams, and your young men shall see visions. Even on the male and female servants in those days I will pour out my Spirit."*

John declares that Jesus has two roles: first, He will take away the sin of the world, this would come through His sacrifice on the cross, and secondly, He will baptize not with water, but with the Holy Spirit.

John 1:29-33: *The next day he saw Jesus coming toward him, and said,* **"Behold, the Lamb of God, who takes away the sin of the world!** *This is he of whom I said, 'After me comes a man who ranks before me, because he was before me.' I myself did not know him, but for this purpose I came baptizing with water, that he might be revealed to Israel." And John bore witness: "I saw the Spirit descend from heaven like a dove, and it remained on him. I myself did not know him, but he who sent me to baptize with water said to me,* **'He on whom you see the**

Spirit descend and remain, this is he who baptizes with the Holy Spirit.'

Jesus commands His disciples to wait upon Him for the promise of the Baptism of the Holy Spirit.

Acts 1:4: *"And while staying with them he ordered them not to depart from Jerusalem, but to wait for the promise of the Father, which, he said, "you heard from me; for John baptized with water, but you will be baptized with the Holy Spirit not many days from now."*

Just moments before Jesus ascended into heaven, He told His disciples that the Spirit would come upon them and they would receive power, and this power would come with a mandate to be witnesses, telling people of Jesus to the ends of the earth (Acts 1:8).

Shortly after, in Acts 2:1-4, when the day of Pentecost arrived, the believers were waiting upon Jesus in the upper room and the Holy Spirit came in the sound of a mighty rushing wind, and tongues of fire appeared on each of their heads.

The Christian life is lifeless without being full of the Holy Spirit and being refilled with the Spirit of God. Paul speaks to this truth in Ephesians,

Ephesians 5:18: *"And do not get drunk with wine, for that is debauchery, but be filled with the Spirit."*

Paul's exhortation to be filled with the Holy Spirit is not a one-time experience, but the word "filled" comes with this idea of being filled over and over. The experience of the early believers speaks to this truth.

Acts 2:4: *"And they were all filled with the Holy Spirit and began to speak in other tongues as the Spirit gave them utterance."*
Acts 4:31: *"And when they had prayed, the place in which they were gathered together was shaken, and they were all filled with the Holy Spirit and continued to speak the word of God with boldness."*
Acts 13:52: *"And the disciples were filled with joy and with the Holy Spirit."*

As followers of Christ, living filled with the Spirit is not an option. If we want to walk in victory over sin, and live empowered to do the things that Jesus did, we need the Spirit.

How to Be Filled With the Holy Spirit
1) Wait Upon the Lord
During your time with the Lord, wait upon Him in silence. Jeremiah writes in **Lamentations 3:25:** *"The Lord is good to those who wait for him, to the soul who seeks him."*

Jesus commands the believers to wait upon the Lord until the Spirit is poured out. Don't leave the upper room until the Spirit comes. (Acts 1:4)

Set aside some time where you do not feel rushed, and where there are no distractions.

2) **Surrender Your Life to Him**
   Matthew 16:24: "Then Jesus told his disciples, *"If anyone would come after me, let him deny himself and take up his cross and follow me."*
   Giving Jesus Lordship of our lives is how we go to the next level in our faith and walk with the Lord. I love what A.W. Tozer says, "God wants the whole person and He will not rest till He gets us in entirety. No part of the man will do."[66]
   I once heard a prayer that has forever marked my life, "Lord, do whatever you want to me, so you can do whatever you want through me." I have prayed this prayer hundreds of times.

3) **Ask For the "Gift" of the Spirit**
   Luke 11:9-13: *"And I tell you, ask, and it will be given to you; seek, and you will find; knock, and it will be opened to you. For everyone who asks receives, and the one who seeks finds, and to the one who knocks it will be opened. What father among you, if his son asks for a fish, will instead of a fish give him a serpent; or if he asks for an egg, will give him a scorpion? If you then, who are evil, know how to give good gifts to your children, how much more will the*

---

[66] A.W. Tozer, The Pursuit of God (Camp Hill, Pennsylvania: WingSpread Publishers, 2006) 101

heavenly Father give the Holy Spirit to those who ask him!"

This is one of my favourite verses in the Bible. Seeking, knocking and asking are all in the context of receiving the Holy Spirit. It is God's desire to pour His Spirit out upon you. ASK HIM!

4) Confession of Sin

It is always good to come before the Lord and ask Him to search our hearts. If the Lord reveals anything to you, praise the Lord, confess it and allow His mercy and forgiveness to wash over you.

1 John 1:9: *"If we confess our sins, he is faithful and just to forgive us our sins and to cleanse us from all unrighteousness."*

The Psalmist asks the question, *"Who can ascend the hill of the Lord?"*

"Who shall ascend the hill of the Lord? And who shall stand in his holy place? He who has clean hands and a pure heart, who does not lift up his soul to what is false and does not swear deceitfully. He will receive blessing from the Lord and righteousness from the God of his salvation. Such is the generation of those who seek him, who seek the face of the God of Jacob. Selah" (Psalm 23:4-6)

5) **Worship Jesus**

   Make much of Jesus. When Jesus is glorified, the Spirit is poured out afresh. Lift your affections to Jesus. The Holy Spirit will fill a room if Jesus is honoured.

   John 7:39: *"Now this he said about the Spirit, whom those who believed in him were to receive, for as yet the Spirit had not been given, because Jesus was not yet glorified."*

   When Jesus is honoured and glorified, it pleases Him to pour out His Spirit upon us. I have led worship in many places and in many different denominations; when Jesus is glorified in purity, you can feel the movement of the Holy Spirit.

6) **Receive By Faith**

   The Lord blesses and rewards those who seek Him; receive the Spirit in faith.

   Hebrews 11:6: *"And without faith it is impossible to please him, for whoever would draw near to God must believe that he exists and that he rewards those who seek him."*

7) **Expect an Encounter**

   When the Father pours out his Spirit on all flesh, there is always a moment of encounter. When the Spirit of God rushes upon you and fills you expect to have an encounter with Jesus. Many have expressed this as overwhelming joy, unspeakable joy, warmth in their inner being. A waterfall of the love of the Father. In the book of Acts when the followers of Jesus were filled with the Spirit there was evidence that followed, there was a moment of encounter. A life lived by the Spirit of God is one that is lived in holiness, according to the fruit of the Spirit. (Gal 5:22)

A Prayer for the Baptism of the Holy Spirit
O Holy Spirit, Come upon me,
Let Your grace and Your glory flow around As I bow at Jesus' feet now
May the fire of heaven flood this holy ground As I worship here in full surrender
Fill my life and lips with highest praise
Come fill me now!
Come fill me now!
O Holy Spirit Come upon me
Till my Jesus - My Lord and Saviour, Jesus - Fills all my ways with his praise
All my days - Jack Hayford[67]

---

[67] Jack Hayford, Baptism With the Holy Spirit. (Grand Rapids, Michigan: Chosen Books, 2004) 51

Recommended Reading

The following list of books are books that have shaped and impacted my life.

The Holy Spirit

Holy Fire - R.T. Kendall
Paul, the Spirit, and the People of God
Fire From Heaven - Harvey Cox
Surprised By the Spirit - Jack Deere
God's Empowering Presence - Gordon D. Fee
The Happiest People on Earth - Demos Shakarian
How to Be Filled with the Holy Spirit - A.W. Tozer
The Beauty of Spiritual Language - Jack Hayford
Baptism With the Holy Spirit - R.A. Torrey
The Hidden Power of Speaking in Tongues - Mahesh Chavda
2000 Years of Charismatic Christianity - Eddie L. Hyatt
Understanding Spiritual Gifts - Sam Storms
Continuous Revival - Norman Grubb
Tongues - Patricia King
Private Prayer Public Power - Ron Smith
Baptism With the Holy Spirit - Jack Hayford
John Wimber's Teaching on the Gift and Gifts of the Holy Spirit - Derek Morphew/Oyvind Nerheim
When Heaven Invades Earth - Bill Johnson
When the Old Becomes New - Dr. Nick Gough
Power From on High - Charles Finney

The Doctrine of the Holy Spirit - George Smeaton[68]
The Essential Guide to Healing
- Bill Johnson and Randy Clark
The Language of Heaven - Sam Storms

Prayer
Why Revival Tarries - Leonard Ravenhill
Revival Praying - Leonard Ravenhill
Teach us To Pray - Corey Russell
The Practice of the Presence of God - Brother Lawrence
Digging the Wells of Revival - Lou Engle
The Gift of Tears - Corey Russell
The Glory Within - Corey Russell
Intimate Friendship with God - Joy Dawson

Biography
John Wimber: His Life and Ministry - Connie Dawson
Pastor Jack - S. David Moore
Rees Howells Intercessor - Norman Grubb
21 Servants of Sovereign Joy - John Piper
The Heavenly Man - Brother Yun
A.W. Tozer: A Twentieth Century Prophet
- David J. Fant Jr.
The Autobiography of George Muller
John Wimber: The Way It Was - Carol Wimber
David Wilkerson - Gary Wilkerson

---

[68] This book is an incredible resource for the work of the Holy Spirit from creation to the return of Christ. However the author, George Smeaton was a Cessationist. He did not believe the gifts of the Spirit were for the church today.

Hearing God's Voice

Is That Really You God - Loren Cunningham
Surprised by the Voice of God - Jack Deere
Ecstatic Prophecy - Stacey Campbell
Love and Prophecy - Dan McCollam
Basic Training for the Prophetic Ministry - Kris Vallotton
Hooked on the Word - Ron Smith
The Seer - James Goll
The God Connection - Bethany Hicks
Basic Training For Prophetic Activation - Dan McCollam
Prophetic Community - Kim Maas
Forever Ruined for the Ordinary - Joy Dawson
The Prophetic Warrior - Emma Stark
Values Matter - Darlene Cuningham
Can You Hear Me? - Brad Jersak
Hearing God - Peter Lord
Modern Prophets - Shawn Bolz
School of the Prophets - Kris Vallotton
Developing Your Prophetic Gifting - Graham Cooke

Fasting

The Hidden Power of Prayer and Fasting
 - Mahesh Chavda
Atomic Power with God thru Fasting and Prayer
 - Franklin Hall
Shaping History Through Prayer and Fasting
 - Derek Prince
The Fast - Lou Engle
A Hunger for God - John Piper

Manufactured by Amazon.ca
Bolton, ON

38346147R00120